WAIT / HEAR

WAIT / HEAR

Recapturing the Lost Art of Hearing God's Voice

ROBBY GALLATY

B&H PUBLISHING®
BRENTWOOD, TENNESSEE

Printed in the United States of America

979-8-3845-1865-5

Published by B&H Publishing Group
Brentwood, Tennessee

Dewey Decimal Classification: 231.74
Subject Heading: GOD / REVELATION
/ PRESENCE OF GOD

Cover design by Tim Green, Tiny Giant Co.
Author photo by Linden Stackley / Long Hollow Church.

1 2 3 4 5 • 29 28 27 26

To the members of Long Hollow Church

Thank you for your patience with me over the past eleven years.

After the revival, you received a new pastor, and I
received a new church—yet none of us had to leave.

CONTENTS

Chapter 1: The Day Revival Came 1

Chapter 2: The More of God You Want 7

Part 1: Stillness

Chapter 3: Where Has All the Silence Gone? 19

Chapter 4: I Just Want to Be Where You Are 31

Part 2: Listening

Chapter 5: And the Word Became Fresh 45

Chapter 6: If You Know What's Good for You 57

Part 3: Rhythm

Chapter 7: The $86,400 Question 71

Chapter 8: Wanting to Be Caught 83

Part 4: Humility

Chapter 9: Are You the Blood Clot to Revival? 97

Chapter 10: You Become What You Behold 109

Part 5: Faith

Chapter 11: A Life Beyond Belief. 123
Chapter 12: This Means War 135

Part 6: Remembrance

Chapter 13: Back to the Future 149
Chapter 14: Thanks a Lot 161

Part 7: Sabbath

Chapter 15: Well-Rested 173
Chapter 16: Where Do We Go from Here? 185

Afterword by Julie Woodruff. 193
Appendix 1: Creating Your Porch 197
Appendix 2: Practical Notes on Selected Disciplines 199
Appendix 3: The H.E.A.R. Journal 203
Acknowledgments 207
Notes 209
About the Author. 213

Chapter 1

THE DAY REVIVAL CAME

It was unusually raw, gray, and chilly, even for a mid-December evening. Light, misty rain had set in for the week, and my every instinct that night, after we'd gotten our boys settled into bed, was to stay comfortably inside the warmth of my house. Instead, I did what I'd been doing almost every night, all spring, all summer, all fall, and now nearly winter.

I went out on the porch, that Tuesday after dark.

And waited to hear from God.

Sunrise broke on the following Sunday morning—December 20, 2020—with the most anticipation I'd felt for a worship service since COVID had knocked us offline, then pushed us online for a big chunk of the year. Our church had already begun meeting again in person long before this Sunday, even though (if you can bear letting yourself think back to it) we were living through a season where the only decisions available to church leaders like me were the kind that made half your people happy, half your people mad. The cultural climate, you'll remember, was truly that divisive.

In fact, before we gathered for worship on that final Sunday before Christmas, after which we wouldn't be meeting together again for several more weeks, we sent out an email urging people to stay home if they felt sick and, if they did attend, to please wear a mask. So, for all those who still felt eager to get out and worship in person, even after accepting these conditions, an equal number of people felt offended. That's just how it was. Some were unwilling to come to church on those terms. I suspected we had probably only set ourselves up for having one of the smallest crowds for a weekend service I'd ever seen since coming to Long Hollow Church as senior pastor five years earlier. And that's exactly what happened.

Except that's not *all* that happened.

Because the porch had happened.

I chose to do something unusual at the end of the first service that morning, something I'd never done before. But I truly believed the Lord had led me to do it. He'd solidified it in my mind and my heart as I sat with Him on the porch the previous Tuesday. And so, despite having no other reason, no plausible reason, for expecting anything special to take place that Sunday, I'd woken up that morning in a state of tangible spiritual confidence. I would've been surprised at that point if, in doing what I thought He'd told me to do, it ended up producing no visible results. It seemed so clear to me now. I was just following His lead. That's all I was trying to do.

But doing what I was about to do made no sense. Because if patterns held, the only people motivated enough to come out to church on a cloudy, COVID-y Sunday were the core groups who were accustomed to being there regularly anyway: our most faithful members, the most seasoned believers. Why should I expect even one of them to feel moved to respond when, after completing my sermon, I walked over to where the baptismal tank was located. Acting on nothing else besides faith-based obedience, I said words like the following:

> Let me ask you something about your baptism. Maybe you're someone who, like me, was sprinkled as an infant, but you've never been baptized after growing up and

> personally believing in Christ as your Savior. Or maybe you walked the aisle as a child, or you first believed on Jesus at summer camp as a teenager, and even though you went down afterward and got wet in a baptistry somewhere (like this one), you know you were not saved when you did it. Your life has proven to you that your real conversion came later, perhaps after years of straying from Him.
>
> If any of those situations describes you, I just wonder if you'd be willing to meet me here—at *this* baptistry, today, on *this* side of your salvation—and take a step of being obedient to Him, by being baptized as a believer.
>
> I know you didn't come here today prepared for this. I know it's unlikely you have a change of clothes with you. I know that. But I want you to know, we've come prepared for *you*—to baptize *you*—if the Lord is calling you to do it.

And with that, I walked off the stage. The band started playing. And nobody moved. Four or five minutes passed. Still nobody was coming. Nobody. I couldn't help thinking I must have somehow really heard wrong on the porch that week and that I really looked foolish just standing there all by myself. With nothing to show for it.

Until one person stood up.

Then two. Then three.

And before we'd concluded the first of our two services that morning, we had baptized twenty-five people, on the spot, who'd come forward testifying to their faith in Christ.

What did this mean? What was God doing?

In between services, I slipped back into my office to eat a little breakfast, when suddenly came a knock at the door.

"Pastor, hate to bother you, but there's a young woman here who watched the first service on her computer at home. She got in her car and drove over, and she wants to know if you'll baptize her."

"You mean, right now?" I said.

He nodded. "Yeah."

"Can we do that?" I asked, half jokingly, looking around from face to face, sort of gauging the room for a response.

We all agreed. There was no reason why not. If she'd come there believing in Christ for her salvation, who was I to withhold water, right? Like Philip and the Ethiopian, in Acts 8.

So I pushed away from the table and made my way back to the worship center, where I met her at the baptistry.

And there, with only the staccato sound of distant conversations echoing through a mostly empty sanctuary, I asked her two questions: (1) "Where are you from?" She said she was from Joelton, a little community about a half hour west of our church. And (2) "Why did you come here to be baptized?"

She answered with the same response that I would hear repeated to me hundreds of times throughout the next eight months, during which as many as 1,600 people would come seeking baptism—not just from nearby little Joelton, Tennessee, but from Maine, from Oregon, from Nevada, from California. From seventeen states, coming in from all over. They'd be like the Harley rider who showed up a little while later, on that same December morning, wearing his biker vest. The second service was soon to begin, so he agreed to stay and worship with us and wait. But when I asked him, like I would later ask all of them, "Why did you come here to be baptized?"—even though I never said, and never did say, to drive in or ride in or fly in or do whatever it took to be here on our physical property in suburban Nashville—he answered by saying what they all would say, almost every time when I asked them that question.

"The Holy Spirit compelled me. I had to come."

The Spirit had led them there. The same Spirit who'd been leading *me*. From the porch to the pulpit. From points all over the map to one pinpoint location. The Spirit was working. The Spirit was calling. And people, in faith, were obeying.

But I can tell you, when the Spirit had prompted me on the porch on Tuesday to make an appeal for spontaneous baptisms the following Sunday, I had my doubts, just being honest with you. I sat on the idea for two days. Not until Thursday and Friday did I dare begin mentioning it to our leadership team, realizing we'd need ample time to prepare ourselves for doing something so unconventional.

Not really until Friday night, as I sat there on the porch again—listening, praying, listening, asking—did I allow myself to believe what I was sure His Spirit had been showing me all along. Because on that night, He put on my heart a specific number of people—100—who would answer His call for baptism when we met that Sunday. *A hundred people.*

Even in believing Him, it still felt like just a ridiculous, impossible number of people to expect. On one day? On one Sunday? Never had we baptized a hundred people in one morning. Who does that? But the Spirit was compelling me, like He would soon be compelling hundreds and hundreds of others, from December until way down into the summer of next year. And by faith, on a Friday night, I just said to Him . . .

Okay.

Okay, Lord. You said it. I'll do it. I even pulled out my phone right then and recorded a video that I immediately sent to the staff. I said, "Sunday is going to be a big day. Get ready for it. I'm believing God that we'll see 100 people baptized. 100! Be praying with me. Believe with me." What were they thinking of me in that moment when they first heard it? I had no idea.

But by the time our final service wrapped up on that December Sunday, guess how many people had passed through the waters of baptism. Ninety-nine. *Not a hundred?* No, not quite. Close. But as someone said to me months later when I was telling this same story that I've been telling you, "You know, I think the only reason you baptized ninety-nine instead of a hundred is because the Lord wanted to tell you there's still one more to go for."

Was there ever.

One after another after another.

And what I needed now—what all of us needed now—was to be sure, before we did another thing, that we were hearing from God about what to do next. Because from what we'd just seen, hearing from God was the only way we were ever going to be doing anything, ever again.

Chapter 2

THE MORE OF GOD YOU WANT

I'd love telling you the reason revival came to our church was because we had reached a level of maturity that God found worthy of His use. Spiritual strength, organizational strength, all the various kinds of naturally generated strength that can make a person, a place, or a thing appear to be outperforming everybody else. Part of me wishes that's the way it works, that the Lord sees us operating at the top of our game, and He therefore deems us qualified to be treated by Him with an elite level of His blessing.

I would say instead, though, that revival came to us as a church, and revival came to me as a leader because we were weak and had nowhere else to go except to Him. *When Jesus is all you have, you realize He is all you need.*

Revival came because we were desperate. Or at least I can tell you this much: The pastor sure was desperate. I was out of sorts and out of solutions—desperate enough to know I had nothing to say if I wasn't hearing from Him.

I'd become senior pastor in the fall of 2015. Long Hollow's longtime pastor, a beloved man, David Landrith, had passed away from cancer the year before, having led the church through nearly two decades of miraculous growth. And not merely numerical growth. You sensed it just walking in—this amazing culture of love for people who were lost and in need of Jesus. The Holy Spirit's presence was palpable from the moment you stepped inside. You could feel the evangelistic heartbeat David had fueled and fostered here. It seemed like just about everybody was eagerly involved and invested in bringing people into a relationship with Christ. And I truly believed, coming into this situation, packed full of so many eager and hungry new Christians, that I knew exactly where to steer it from there.

In both churches I'd pastored so far, I'd tried to duplicate the method of disciple-making that had been modeled for me personally. It's how the Lord had grown me up so quickly as a twenty-six-year-old baby believer, rescued from drugs, alcohol, debt, and disaster, and just about everything else a guy could gain and lose in such a short amount of life. By God's grace, I had seen this emphasis on discipleship take hold in every church I'd led—the power of following Christ's command to "go, therefore, and make disciples" (Matt. 28:19). I'd seen people mature. I'd seen whole families transformed. I'd seen addicts set free and marriages restored. God had blessed those churches beyond measure. Slow growth, but steady growth, the kind where the roots grow deep and the faithful grow tall. The fruit of spiritual multiplication. Generation after generation.

That's what I prayed for and envisioned, a plan I was simply transferring now into a new and bigger environment. Because I knew I was good at this. I could do it. I'd done it before. All I had to do was just do it again. And everything would be great. And, of course, everybody would love me for it. (Can't say I wasn't motivated by that too.)

But, man, did I underestimate what can happen when a big, 6'6", deep-voiced, high-intensity presence comes in, acting like he knows everything nobody else knows about growing a church.

I was convinced my plan would work. It had *always* worked. And the people at Long Hollow, to their credit, let me do it my way for a while. They tolerated me as the new guy, with all my preaching and prioritizing and programming the church for discipleship—which we should have done, and which we still do.

But over time, the emphasis I was forcing down on them from above led to a lot of people thinking all I cared about was getting Christians into small, intimate discipleship groups and that I didn't care too much about the lost, at least not as much as the pastor who'd been leading them all these years. And some of them were already telling me, if I didn't make some adjustments to myself and my leadership style, the next thing I was going to be losing would be the church.

By five years into my ministry here, which you'd think would be enough time for me to feel like I was rowing the boat, I was sinking like a rock. Spiritually, emotionally, mentally, even physically. And our church's weekly attendance was sinking right down *with* me. From 6,700 or so to around 3,400. Just about in half. And a percentage of that remaining number were probably only still there because they hated changing churches more than they disliked *me*.

Then came COVID.

And the man who was pastoring their church came completely apart.

Desperation can lead you to do desperate things. Ask me how I know. Or maybe you don't need me to ask because you already know what I'm talking about. Maybe you're up to your neck right now in desperation, and you're splashing around for any sort of life preserver you can grab onto to get back to solid ground, to feel spiritually reconnected with God again.

How would you describe what your desperation feels like today? Is it burnout? Just way too much stuff coming at you? At work, at home. In your mind, in your body. You wear the virtue of being overworked like a badge of honor on your chest. You're tired—*so* tired—but you're afraid to let yourself slow down for a minute because the thought of getting any further behind makes you feel more overloaded than ever.

Or is it maybe that feeling of being lost at sea, just floating without direction. You started out thinking you knew where you were headed. All your expectations were still out in front of you. But then something shifted. Something threw your plans off course. People keep looking to you now to know what to do because that's your role in the church or your family or wherever you lead. And you want to do it because you believe you should. But you don't know how you can. Because you don't even know what you should be doing yourself.

And you're desperate. Maybe it's from failure. Or from crippling bouts with fear. Or financial trouble and all the pressures and worries that can wake you up in a cold sweat in the middle of the night. Maybe it's from losses in your health or your relationships or from a season of real uncertainty at work, the kind that feels like if the worst-case scenario comes about, it could just collapse all around you at a moment's notice.

Or maybe you're like me. You're a ministry leader. And the only persona you've ever really played is the one where nothing is ever allowed to come up at any time that you're not supposed to be able to figure out or handle. Maybe not perfectly but eventually. If they just give you time.

I'd tell you I used to pride myself on that. I felt inspired by a good challenge. I always wanted to be the person who could do the impossible. Maybe other people couldn't, but I could. Before coming to Christ, my motto was, "If it's meant to be, it's up to me." Tell me I couldn't achieve something, that I couldn't put a plan together for it and accomplish it, and here's what I'd tell you: You should plan on being amazed at how anyone, having this many things on his plate, could somehow pull off another one as well. And could do it so well.

That was me. The one who knew what to do and made it look easy. After all, I'm a pastor. Desperate people are who I *deal with*, not who I *am*. I'm paid *not* to be desperate, never to look rushed or overwhelmed—to know what the Bible says, to know who God is, to know where He is, and to keep my cool while I'm waiting for Him. People come asking *me* questions. Desperate people. Not the other way around. I can't afford to be desperate.

Or that's what I thought.

Until I was.

And, believe me, I was desperate.

If this was what it was like to be in ministry—pastoring a declining church, something I'd never experienced in all my years of full-time service—I was so done with it. I was sick of trying to keep everybody pleased around me, only to be told how far short I was falling of doing what they expected.

I was trying my best. And yet I was being constantly critiqued and criticized for doing what I thought was the right way, the best way, to get our church growing and thriving again. *I cared about revival, but all I could do was just focus on survival.* This was not how I saw my life playing out when I'd been given the opportunity to serve God at this incredible place. I wished for more. And now, truth be told, I was sometimes wishing for the exit door.

For two months after being told the church was falling out underneath me, I committed every available breakfast and lunch slot in my schedule for meeting with a revolving door of concerned church members. I asked them, one after another, to help me see what I obviously wasn't seeing, to point out for me the blind spots that were hindering me from being the pastor they felt like I needed to be.

I'd sit there with both my heart and my notebook lying wide open. *I have no other agenda*, I'd say to them, *except for being here to learn*. I wanted the truth. I wanted to know. And I'm sure it was valuably important for me to hear every nugget of honest feedback that they dared to address with me.

But after a while, it just left me reeling. Could all of it really be true? About me? Successful me? About the megachurch pastor in me? I had to remind myself I wasn't as good as I thought, but surely I wasn't as bad as others said I was.

It was brutal. It was painful. And I don't know why I didn't give up right then because I know I felt like it. And from what people were telling me, I wasn't the only one who shared that sentiment.

But somehow, one night, I ended up out on my front porch. Just me. Just sitting there. Just staring off into the distance and darkness. Not knowing what was out there. Little did I know, in that desperate moment, that it would lead to ten months of similar moments, every night without fail—right there, in that chair. Right there, with that view. Right there, where I would finally get quiet and still enough to listen to the God I'd talked about so much and so often with such authority for most of my adult life. Though maybe I hardly even knew Him.

Because maybe I'd hardly ever slowed down enough to hear Him.

And that's what brings you to this book. A book I didn't want to write, at least not in the sense of previous books I've written. I think I always felt confident in ministry—the Bible guy, the discipleship guy, the PhD graduate. And I think there's possibly truth to the idea that maybe one of the reasons God would send revival to "the discipleship guy" is because He knew our church wouldn't let people go out the back door as quickly as they'd come in the front. We may not have discipled all of those He brought to us during that revival, but we've certainly tried. And we are certainly still trying.

But in this book about a desperate time in my life, and about the desperate times in all our lives, the best I can do is to approach it not as an expert but as a learner. The learner I'm still becoming. The learner I hope I will always be. I've never felt less qualified to put words on the page, and yet I've never felt more determined, more driven—more *desperate*—to walk together with you under an open sky, with open hands before our ever-present Lord, and wait with open ears to hear what His Holy Spirit would say to us.

So prepare to get personal with me. Because I'm prepared to get personal with you. And prepare to know God in ways that stretch the tight controls of experience and education, of anything you've set up as a boundary to limit His open access to your deepest places. Because the right response to seasons of doubt and desperation, if you want God to do with them what He intends in your life, is to get more real with Him and with others than you've ever been before.

Oh, and if you're truly as desperate as you say (and I believe you are), prepare to join me in being ready to change.

The entire Christian life is about change. At salvation, you and I became a "new creation" in Christ—"the old has passed away, and see, the new has come!" (2 Cor. 5:17). And at every step, "we all, with unveiled faces" are meant to be "looking as in a mirror at the glory of the Lord" so that we are *continually being changed*—"transformed into the same image from glory to glory; this is from the Lord who is the Spirit" (2 Cor. 3:18).

We are not meant to stay the same. God meets every one of us where we are, but He doesn't leave us where we were. We keep following the same Lord, of course, and we seek Him through the same Word, and we worship the same Father and King who patiently hears our prayers and truthfully discerns our hearts. But He loves to do new things. And He loves when His children sing a new song. He loves that look in our eyes when, after we've tested again the fortifications of our faith, we more clearly resemble the Son, who never allowed hollow, earthly traditions to interfere with His passion for staying completely aligned with heaven.

And that means *hearing* from heaven. Listening for the voice of God. Not just the cerebral exercise of knowing things about Him but the essential experience of personally relating with Him. In the quiet. In the questions.

As I sat on the porch for ten months—much of it in silence and solitude—the Holy Spirit of God spoke something into my heart that has already altered me forever. "Robby," He seemed to say, "you have as much of Me as you want. And I want you to know, there is so much more."

More of His power.

More of His companionship.

More of His personal speaking voice.

More of *Him*, and of all the ways He wants to communicate His heart with us if we, His dearly loved children, will simply draw close enough to hear.

We shouldn't be surprised by that. "Draw near to God," the Bible says, "and he will draw near to you" (James 4:8). "Seek, and you will find" (Matt. 7:7). "Call to me and I will answer you and tell you great and incomprehensible things you do not know" (Jer. 33:3). But not if we insist on staying the same. Not if we avoid letting him turn the spotlight on our most undetected or untouchable sins. And certainly not if we continue to respond to Him the same way we did when we lacked the desperation for doing much more than feigning an interest in Him.

I'd had enough of that. Haven't *you*? I needed more than that.

And, praise God, I am still reaping the benefits that grow out of that. I'm not sure I believed He could do it (or *would* do it) for someone like me, a guy who'd always had so much to say but still had so much to learn. Until He just did. Until He came and met me, night after night, on the porch. That's when everything changed.

Not just for me.

It's what I'm praying now for you.

The following chapters contain a number of disciplines the Holy Spirit brought to my attention to get my desperate heart receptive to the direction He longs to provide. Some of the things I'll be talking about will likely be unfamiliar to you. Many of them were unfamiliar to me. But in my quest for a new beginning with God, my journey led me deep into the thoughts and words and practices of believers from the dark ages of church history, some of whom I was taught in seminary to avoid at all costs. I'm not saying I completely agree with every tenet of doctrine held by every person whose name I've included here. But growing up around the Cajun restaurants and dinner tables of south Louisiana, I became a practitioner of eating the fish and spitting out the bones. Just because you're not a fan of everything the chef puts on the menu, you can still walk away knowing you had a really good meal.

All that to say, I'm not placing into your hands the definitive guidebook to all things spiritual. I would never want my experience to frame or overshadow your own encounter with God. Few things quench the Spirit more than the idolatry of human methods. But I can promise you I've field-tested these principles and activities I'm writing about. And if you've finally heard enough of all that inner condemnation of yours and the mass confusion of the world, I believe you're ready to try some things that can cultivate an ear for hearing from God.

Care to join me?

I'll be waiting on the porch for you.

At nightfall on that miraculous Sunday in December 2020, after a full morning and afternoon of baptizing ninety-nine people who'd publicly demonstrated their faith in Christ, I slipped back out on the porch again. My gratitude had no lid, no limit. After what we'd all seen the Spirit do in our midst that day, I could not hold back the tears. Just weeping. Shaking with emotion. It had been so supernatural, so beyond anything I'd ever seen—and, believe me, as a recovered addict, I'd seen a lot.

The evening air around me felt alive with this fearful sense of His holiness. I was sitting on holy ground. I'd done nothing; He'd done everything. And it left me trembling now, thinking how close I could've come to tuning out His voice the night before, simply because what He'd said to me had not been in keeping with my experience or my natural train of thought.

Yet even then, even feeling the complete God-ness of it all, normal human Robby defaulted into assuming the astounding events of that day were a one-time, incredible outpouring of His Spirit that, thank God, we'd been there to witness. Because, surely, nothing so spiritually mind-blowing would ever happen like that again, to that degree, in my lifetime. I remember resting my head back, gazing up into the night sky, and thinking, *Man, one day I'll be telling my grandkids about this.* The thought was so sweet that I allowed my eyes to close in meditation, in keeping with my sense of worship.

But no sooner had the stage darkened in my mind than the Lord sparked it to light with what I can only describe to you as a waking vision. I saw before me, against my closed eyelids, a scene of heavy raindrops descending from the heavens and landing on the ground, the kind of rain that signals the approach of a torrential downpour. And in my spirit echoed a pulsating thought that appeared to match the images I believed His Spirit was showing me. These words: *This is just the beginning.*

Just . . . the beginning.

It sure was. Trust me when I tell you, the year that followed at Long Hollow is still alive to tell the story that He began in us when we, and when I, finally got serious about hearing Him.

What if your own desperation is "just the beginning" of the revival you need as well? What if being beat down by burnout is possibly the one thing that finally gets you back to doing the one thing—the one thing that was supposed to be the One Thing all along. Because when you and I are down to nothing, God is always up to something.

And that, my friend, is always a good thing.

Part I

STILLNESS

Chapter 3

WHERE HAS ALL THE SILENCE GONE?

All of humanity's problems stem from man's inability to sit quietly in a room alone.[1]

Blaise Pascal

Desperation has a sound, a tempo, a language.

It's like a drumbeat of noise—incessant, aggressive, intrusive.

I doubt you need me to describe it for you. Close your eyes and you'll hear it. Not just the noise around you but the noise inside you. The noise of stress. The noise of opinions, both yours and others. The noise of regret. The noise of shame. The noise of questions with no reasonable answers. The noise of problems parading as impossibilities.

And all this noise would be inescapable if not for a gift from God that can restore a measure of peace to our blood pressure and the hope of revival to our hearts. Except that one of the few things most of us find more unendurable than the pounding headache of noise between our temples is the dread of being left alone with its potential remedy.

I introduce you now to *silence.*

A guy in our church, during one of my lowest times, warned me I needed to slow down. He could tell I was running at a frenetic pace, which was kind of my normal pace, but he was right in saying to me that it was an unsustainable pace. "The thing you need more than anything," he told me, "is to learn how to be silent and still before the Lord."

My first thought upon hearing his counsel was not like, *Give me a break*. Because I actually tended to agree with him. It's just that whenever I would read books on spiritual disciplines, and I would come to the parts that talked about silence, stillness, and solitude, an immediate switch would go off in my mind that said, *No way, that stuff's not for me.*

So here's where I should probably introduce myself to you a little more completely. Anyone who knows me knows I have ADHD. Not just by casual observation but by official diagnosis. My mind is always racing. It's how my brain chemistry works. I could be completely immersed in one of my favorite hobbies today, but check back in with me a few months from now, and I'll be off doing something else. And not just dabbling in it but deep in it. Like, I won't just be twisting the dials on a few pieces of HAM radio equipment that I ordered, but I'll have studied up and taken the courses and earned the highest level of license a radio operator can achieve, faster than any sane person would dream of doing it. I'm basically addicted to learning and doing. It's crazy, living like this.

But when this friend of mine said what he said to me, about slowing down, it was one of the first times I thought I should try it. I should try silence. I should try stillness. I mean, I'd tried a lot of things, and nothing seemed to be working. Whatever I was doing was getting me nowhere but into more trouble. Maybe a new emphasis on spending dedicated time in silence would help me. What if I gave it fifteen minutes?

That's what I told myself. My goal, the first time I stepped out onto the porch in March 2020, was to commit a solid *fifteen minutes* waiting in silence on the Lord.

Now think with me how quickly the average fifteen minutes travel across the backdrop of your average day. When you need to go somewhere and you've only got fifteen minutes to get ready, you can barely throw on your clothes and find your keys and wallet before those fifteen minutes are gone. Where'd they go? Fifteen minutes sail by in a flash. But make the deliberate effort to sit down to quiet your mind and your heart, with nothing else to occupy your attention, and you'd swear your watch must have stopped. Everything else is in motion—your eyes, your feet, your hands, your position in your seat. Why is the time suddenly going so slow?

This should be easy, just sitting still. Why is it so hard? Why can't I control myself?

A study published in the journal *Science* reported the results of hundreds of volunteers who were asked to spend between six and fifteen minutes sitting alone in a single room with nothing but their own thoughts to keep them company.[2] And in every case, whether the experiment was conducted in a classroom setting or even in the comfort of a person's own home, more than half of the respondents described the experience as being unenjoyable. If given a book, it might have been different, they said. If allowed to listen to music, maybe it would've been okay then. But just sitting there? Quietly? With nothing to do?

Intolerable.

To test the far reaches of their findings, the researchers played with leaving a button in the room that participants were told would give them an electric shock if pushed. Though all of them said ahead of time they would pay money if it would keep them from having an electrical surge coursing through their body, a "shocking" number of them—too bored to resist after ten minutes of this torment—pressed the button anyway. (Mostly the men. Not surprised.)

But after having endured my own first fifteen minutes of ADHD silence on the porch, I can honestly say I get where they're coming from. It was kind of more than I could stand. No people. No music. No phone. No nothing.

Does just the idea of it make you uncomfortable, the way it did me? If it does, you're not alone. Abba Agathon was one of the "desert fathers," they're called—Christian ascetics from the first few centuries AD who practiced rigorous self-discipline, self-denial, and renunciation of worldly comforts and pleasures in pursuit of spiritual purification and a deeper union with God. Yet even he struggled so mightily to cultivate silence in his life that he kept a stone in his mouth for three years until he mastered the practice. Dallas Willard, too, the late author and philosopher who wrote the book *Hearing God*, identified silence and solitude as the most challenging spiritual disciplines in the Christian life. And if he hadn't said it first, I'd be saying it now.

Yet when it comes to what our desperate selves need most, it doesn't matter what he said or what I say. The only thing that matters is what God says. And silence, contrary to popular desire, is God's native language. We hear Him best when we're listening quietly.

Ask Elijah. I bet you know the story. From the bowels of depression and disillusionment, he dared respond to God's command to "go out and stand on the mountain in the LORD's presence" (1 Kings 19:11). And despite wind and fire and earthquake and all the trademark conditions that indicated God was in the house, the Bible says He was not. He was not in the commotion. He was not in the noise. His "voice," said the Spirit through the writer of 1 Kings, was instead "a soft whisper" (v. 12). Elijah heard him not in the loud but in the quiet.

As did many others in Scripture, who knew how the Lord is best heard.

> Habakkuk: "The LORD is in his holy temple; let the whole earth be silent in his presence" (Hab. 2:20).
>
> Zephaniah: "Be silent in the presence of the Lord GOD, for the day of the LORD is near" (Zeph. 1:7).
>
> Zechariah: "Let all humanity be silent before the LORD, for from his holy dwelling he has roused himself" (Zech. 2:13).

I can even take you back to creation. The silence of creation. "The earth was formless and empty, darkness covered the surface of the watery depths, and the Spirit of God was hovering over the surface of the waters" (Gen. 1:2). Can you hear it? The silence? The intense, palpable quiet? Before the stars blazed in the sky, before the planets spun in space, the whole idea of a created universe waited in expectant silence—waited for the word of God to paint the worlds into existence. Everything sprang forth from silence. In silence is where we hear His voice.

Which begs the question: *If silence is God's native language, why do we so rarely speak it?*

Desperation cries out for resolution. We want this situation resolved. We want to get back to where we were. Hopefully *better* than we were, but definitely not as bad as we're doing right now. Not as far away from God as our heart feels. With so little time to make up the distance.

And so, as determined believers, we're willing to back up for a minute. Take our lumps, take our medicine. Even take these fifteen minutes out in the fresh air to clear our head and catch a deep breath. But on the other side of our silent sacrifice, we expect an answer to be waiting there for us once we've put in the effort. That's how we want God to work. If we put in the time, we want to get something in return. And the quicker, the better.

The Lord, knowing us as He does, allows many of our spiritual disciplines to operate in this fashion. When we seek Him in His Word, we typically receive the benefit of being enlightened, convicted, directed by His truth. When we pursue Him in prayer, desiring Him to act, we watch and wait for His response. When we share Christ with someone, our hope and dream is that they eventually say yes to Him. And especially if we go a step further—like, let's say we bite off a more costly discipline, like fasting—we do it expecting some sort of breakthrough from

God. And He seems to love giving us that. He is so gracious with His good gifts.

Built into most of these experiences with Him is a law of reciprocity. *I* do something; *God* does something. We come to Him expecting to receive. And I think that's okay. There's nothing inherently impure behind that motivation. But just because we've received blessing from Him doesn't mean we've heard from Him. Maybe we got what we came for, but did we get what *He* came for?

I've come to believe that's what silence is for.

Early on, when I went on the porch each night, I went expecting God to speak. I didn't know if He would spell out a Hebrew word for me in the pattern of the constellations. I didn't know if the heavens would suddenly erupt with all the booming vibrance of a godlike megaphone. The truth is, He did speak to me eventually. But not in the way I was expecting.

What I'm about to say might scare you away, but I'm just telling you what happened. I kept going out on that porch night after night, week after week, month after month. I didn't just sit there like a stone. To set the record straight, I'm not advocating navel-gazing. It's true I'm not as weirded out as I used to be by the mystical and the unexplainable, but I promise you I haven't tossed all my discernment out the window. You may not agree with me at every turn, which is fine. Please, though, hear me saying something else too: I don't want to spend more time coming up with arguments against everything that makes me uncomfortable than confronting my own unwillingness to do uncomfortable things. Fair enough?

After a month of practicing this discipline—only a month!—my fifteen minutes had become thirty, then forty-five, ultimately up to about an hour and a half. Every night. Ninety minutes of silence. And though I was still compelled to keep it up, and though I was beginning to experience a number of spiritual changes in my life, I remember the specific hour, around three months in, preparing to go back inside for the night, when I said aloud to the Lord, "What was that, God? I got nothing from being out here."

Boom.

Instantly, a coherent thought formed in my mind, and I could tell in my spirit that it was a response from the Holy Spirit. "Robby, you didn't get nothing; you got everything—because I got *you*, and you got *Me*."

And from that moment, I knew. It had taken three months of breaking down my discomfort, but the Lord had gotten through to me. There's something in the practice of silence and solitude that invites you back behind the wall of that law of reciprocity, back to the place where He can transform you into someone who is content and satisfied just in coming to Him, just in being with Him, even if He appears to be giving you nothing back.

Hearing the thought of those words from Him—and, I mean, I still get chills thinking about them—it reoriented my expectations each night as I sat alone silently with Him on the porch. It wasn't something I didn't already know; it was something I'd just stopped keeping in front of me. And here it is: If all I wanted was His hand (what He could give me) and not His face, I'd be left getting neither. But if I truly sought His face (who He is) and not His hand, I'd get both.

God didn't want something from me. He just wanted *me*. And although He doesn't need anything from anyone, He enjoys spending time with us. He desired my company. *And I bet He misses your company as well.*

It's hard, though, getting past your inner rebellion to it, the part of you that believes sitting in silence is a big waste of time. I promise you, if you ever consistently attempt it, as I'm proposing to you here,* you will encounter this objection on an almost everyday basis. How it's too slow. How it's too boring. How it

* See Appendix 1, "Creating Your Porch: Setting Up a Space for Silence."

doesn't feel like it's accomplishing anything. How you don't have time just to sit around like this. In my case, it took months before I could encounter the silence without pulling equally hard to get away from it.

To be silent is to become intently aware of all the ways we are *not* silent, all the ways we don't *want* to be silent. And our attraction to all this noise, all the time, is our way of convincing ourselves we have more to gain from being surrounded by constant sound than from living at a quieter volume and a less hurried pace.

That's funny, though, because it's certainly not what the Bible says. If anything, God's encouragement to us in Scripture is to quiet down, slow down, and wait on Him. "Be silent before the LORD and wait expectantly for him" (Ps. 37:7). "You will be delivered by returning and resting; your strength will lie in quiet confidence" (Isa. 30:15). "The LORD will fight for you," Moses said to the children of Israel, squeezed tight between the Egyptian soldiers and the Red Sea, but if you expect to see Him do it, "you must be quiet" and watch Him work (Exod. 14:14).

Be quiet *first*.

Then the things of God start happening.

Several months after I'd started sitting on the porch every night, I had to go out of town for a couple of days, where I wasn't able to spend the same amount of time waiting silently before the Lord like I'd normally been doing. The next day after I got back, I was involved in a meeting at church, after which a lead team member on our staff pulled me aside and said, "Hey, man, you seem a little agitated today. Are you sitting at night with the Lord still?"

It had become that noticeable. God had been making me different in the silence, more than I even realized. And without it? Look what was happening: I was leaking back into being the same stressed-out guy who'd gotten me so out of whack to begin with.

But we don't see it. We don't see how diseased we've become by being allergic to silence. The noise has blinded us to our condition. Or, I guess, deafened us to it.

In a recent survey, 70 percent of Europeans said being "loud" is the most identifying trait of American tourists.[3] Yet we somehow don't think of ourselves that way, and we don't recognize how significantly it impacts how we think, act, and live. We don't seem able to discern the connection between our lack of steadiness and our lack of stillness.

As strange as it sounds to say, noise is a silent killer.

Before I share with you one of the practices God has used in helping me develop an ear for hearing the accent of the Holy Spirit, let's start with an illustration or two for how silence affects your soul.

Imagine dipping a clear glass container into a river, pulling up a pitcher full of murky water. Setting it down on the shore, you wouldn't be able to see through the glass for all the dirt, algae, sand, and debris swirling around inside. But if you leave it alone long enough, all the sediment slowly settles to the bottom. By waiting, you're eventually able to peer clearly through the glass. Where everything was muddy before, now you see.

That's the work of silence in your heart, your mind, your spirit. It's kind of like the ginger that comes on the tray when a server brings sushi to your table. By placing it on your tongue between tasting the different rolls, the ginger cleanses your palate so you can enjoy the full, rich flavor of the next one. Silence cleanses our spiritual palates so we can digest and process new experiences and information. It transforms the place we're sitting—*any* place—into a sacred space with God. And it prepares us for being open to hear what He's wanting to reveal to us.

But, again, I'm not talking about emptying your mind to absorb the spirit of silence and allow your soul to escape the body. I'm talking about quieting the nonstop noise around you so you can hear the Lord when He speaks. Biblical meditation is not *mental passivity* where you flatline all your thinking. Rather, it is *mental focus* on the Word of God, the promises of God, the presence of God. The best way to overcome your resistance to sitting in silence with Him is to formulate a reliable plan that guides you into it.

So here's mine. And I discovered it in the writings of James Finley, a novice who studied under Thomas Merton in the Abbey of Gethsemani in Kentucky. (And, please, I implore you, if your doctrinal antennae will not let you proceed beyond the sentence I just wrote, please wait with me long enough to hear the Scriptures you adore carry you closer to the God you adore.)

Psalm 46:10 (KJV): "Be still, and know that I am God." Think of the words as a tuning fork, helping to realign your heart to Him. It's a simple practice. Just repeat the words of the verse and pause to let its invitation linger around you. Then next, remove one word, or one thought, from the end of the verse, and repeat it again:

"Be still, and know that I am God."

(Pause)

"Be still, and know that I am . . ."

(Pause)

"Be still, and know . . ."

(Pause)

"Be still . . ."

(Pause)

"Be . . ."

"Be."

Allow that final word to resonate in your mind. Not just resonate there but remind you that you are not primarily a human producer of product but a human being made in the image of God. You are not here to *do* something for Him but to experience *being* with Him. Your purpose is not to get something from God but to *be* who He made you to be.

And His Word says to wait on Him. To "be still" before Him.

I repeat this pattern every time I sit down in silence with Him.* I love it so much. Sometimes I'll work through it differently than at other times. Sometimes I'll stop and explore more deeply the last word of each line. Like, "I am"—what does "I am" mean? *It means You are always with me. You are closer to me than my own breath. You are here with me now. Though I can only see You with the eyes of my faith, You are here. You ARE. The "I Am."*

So it's not a rote repeating of words for me. It's instead become a familiar front porch that welcomes me to sit down. The silence of saying it, or just thinking it, slows down the rpm of my soul. It helps me dwell on Him, on the truer-than-true reality that I am right now in His presence.

"Be still."

"And know."

"I am God."

To do otherwise—to keep moving, to keep talking, to keep thinking I know most everything about Him already, to keep operating as though I am functionally God myself—is to never really know what being in His presence is like. To never really know Him. Or what He's thinking. Or what He's saying.

* See Appendix 2 for additional tips on how to make the most of this practice.

Thomas Merton, who I just mentioned, was a brilliantly articulate writer who became a Trappist monk as a young man in the 1940s. He captured well the aversion of most churchgoers and church leaders to being still in God's presence:

> Interior solitude is impossible for them. They fear it. They do everything they can do to escape it. What is worse, they try to draw everyone else into activities as senseless and devouring as their own. They are great promoters of useless work. They love to organize meetings and banquets and conferences and lectures. They print circulars, write letters, talk for hours on the telephone in order that they may gather a hundred people together in a large room where they will all fill the air with smoke and a great deal of noise and roar at one another and clap their hands and stagger home at last patting one another on the back with the assurance that they have done great things to spread the Kingdom of God.[4]

But have they? Have we?

Or have we only hidden ourselves behind the raucous noise of our souls and our habits, even the hardworking beehive of our good intentions, and succeeded mostly at just confusing ourselves about whose voice is the most important here?

In the wake of revival, people would often ask me for the secret behind the transformation they'd seen in our church. *What did you do? What steps did you take?*

The answer is as simple as it is difficult. We got quiet before the Lord. We sat beholding His glory without an agenda. We committed ourselves to unhurried, uninterrupted times with Jesus, and we got to know the Holy Spirit on a personal level. Rather than continuing to swim in a sea of words, we parked ourselves in His presence. And there, where we began to grasp again the grand reality of the One who invites us into relationship with Him, we heard His voice. In the silence.

Chapter 4

I JUST WANT TO BE WHERE YOU ARE

One of the great uses of Twitter and Facebook will be to prove at the Last Day that prayerlessness was not from lack of time.[5]

John Piper

I think all of us know people who relate to Christ at such an expressive level of openness and spiritual freedom that, though they tend to inspire us, they can also kind of horrify us. We're not quite sure if they are legitimately that much closer to Jesus than we are or if they're just . . . weird. But part of us can't help wondering: Are we missing something? Because they seem to *have* something. Something vibrant. Something deep. Something noticeably present and alive.

Something that maybe we don't.

That's how I've sometimes felt whenever I've read or heard about some of the voices throughout church history, both ancient and modern, who've been loosely labeled as *mystics*. Christian mystics. They're easy to criticize because we're so accustomed to Christian lifestyles that look different from theirs—lives that are more compatible with society, lives more closely guarded against extremes, lives more carefully edited and curated for public consumption. But even if you consider the teachings and examples of the mystics to be sketchy or unwise or even dangerously unorthodox—which, I'll admit to you, some of it can be—you can't help noticing how their union with the presence of God was, and is, often more real and experiential than all our training and caution and rightness will sometimes allow us to be.

We must resist the crippling effects of an autobiographical ministry mindset that plagues most pastors and many believers—the posture that says, "If I haven't experienced it firsthand, it can't be true or real or biblical." I've learned that God will not be put into a box. He will do what He wants, when He wants, how He wants, without our input or approval.

Evelyn Underhill, a British writer from the early twentieth century who wrote widely on the spiritual life, told of the patterns she observed from studying the early mystics of the faith. How did they keep their walk with Christ from becoming mechanical and routine? How were they able, seemingly more than others, to live each moment so abundantly aware of the abiding presence of God?

She summarized her answer this way: "This happened to them," this experience of living moment by moment in the presence of God . . .

> not because He loved and attended to them more than He does to us, but because they loved and attended to Him more than we do.[6]

They desired God more than they desired anyone or anything else. And they spent the greater part of their lives in an ongoing, communicative relationship with Him, as if the things their faith told them to believe about Him were actually true. That He was actually here. And that He wanted to be with them.

And from my seat on the porch, as I was slowly becoming more aware of His desire for my company, He was performing a work in my heart that made me feel that same way, making me crave His presence more each day, more than I think I'd ever felt before. This revival in me was not the result of any striving or moving or creating or speaking of mine. It was all His doing. All I was giving Him was myself. But in this silent exchange, He was causing me to unlearn my old perception of how a person encounters God. Rather than by implementing another program, rather than by memorizing another method, He makes Himself known to us by our simply making the space to spend time with Him.

Just to be. To be still. With God.

In His presence.

Like you, most likely, I grew up watching *Mister Rogers' Neighborhood*, one of the staples of children's TV viewing for several decades. Fred Rogers, who was a Presbyterian minister before becoming a beloved "television neighbor" to generations of little children (and their parents), had a way of speaking into the camera as if he were your personal friend.

In the 2019 movie *A Beautiful Day in the Neighborhood*, a reluctant reporter is tasked with interviewing Mr. Rogers on the set of his program for a magazine article. But the session goes badly, or at least goes differently from what the reporter expected, because instead of letting him stick to the usual question-and-answer format, Mr. Rogers does more of the interviewing than the interviewer does. The curious interchange makes the man uncomfortable. He doesn't like having his own life exposed or brought out into the open like this. Their time together runs out, and he's left without having gathered any insights on this person that he can turn into a story. Frustrated, he walks away. Irritated. Really irritated. He can't believe a guy who comes across as so nice and approachable on TV is so meddlesome in person.

The next day, the phone rings in the reporter's apartment. It's Fred Rogers, calling to continue their conversation that had become interrupted the previous day. The man doesn't really feel like talking, having gotten a bad impression from their earlier meeting. But he hesitatingly decides to hear him out. After all, that's what this whole exercise was supposed to be—finding out from his subject what he finds important about his television work and the mission behind it.

"Do you know what the most important thing in the world is to me, right now?" Mr. Rogers asks, in his unmistakably sincere tone of voice.

Uh, again, I'm the one who's supposed to be asking the questions here, but—"No," the reporter says. "No, I don't."

"Talking on the telephone to *you*."

And as hard as it is to believe, this is somewhat descriptive of how God feels about *us*. He wants to share His heart with us. By His love, by His will, and by the glory He receives from working through us—through *us*, the unworthy recipients of His grace—He focuses His attention on us to engage us in relationship. As if we're the most important thing in the world to Him right now. The only question is, Why would the most important thing in *our* world, in *our* hearts, at any moment of every day—right now—not be experiencing His presence, listening to Him, wanting to hear what our Father wants to say to us? And if it's not, why not?

It's because for people who should desire being in His presence more than we desire anyone or anything else, we are consumed instead with being in the presence of *everything* else.

We may be desperate for Him, but, boy, are we ever distracted from being with Him.

You've heard Jesus's parable of the sower, probably a hundred times. I'm assuming you've always believed—as I did and preached about it for years—that His main point in telling this story was to illustrate how evangelism works. A sower "went out to sow" (Matt. 13:3)—to spread abroad "the word about the kingdom" (v. 19)—and the seed landed in different types of soil. Three times out of four, the person given the opportunity to receive the seed, to receive God's gift of salvation, turned it away instead. Therefore, these are the rates of return we should generally expect whenever we share the gospel with the unsaved. It's a one-in-four proposition. Some receive Him, but most reject

Him because the makeup of their "soil" is resistant to the gospel. That's the popular interpretation of this parable.

But after carefully considering the cultural context of the story and the audience to whom Jesus was speaking, I have changed my perspective. No longer do I think His purpose was to show His followers the difference between people who are going to heaven and people who are not. I now believe His story is a mirror for us as believers to hold up in front of our own faces, helping us diagnose the condition of our soul. Because even in being a person whom God has already saved, our lives can look like *all* the different kinds of soils, sometimes in the space of one weekend. Hard-hearted, shallow, overcrowded, receptive. Yet only one of those types of soil—the "good" soil (vv. 8, 23)—gives the seed what's required for bearing fruit in it.

I'll circle back to this parable again in the next chapter because its imagery is so vital, I think, in helping us recalibrate our relationship with God. But for now, I want to spotlight only one of the soils Jesus described: the ground that was tangled with thorns. "This is one who hears the word," Jesus said, "but the worries of this age and the deceitfulness of wealth choke the word, and it becomes unfruitful" (v. 22).

These are the distracted hearts. And all too often these are *our* hearts. This is the heart of someone who's become a cyber-zombie tethered to his or her digital devices. This is the heart that keeps us constantly swiping up and swiping down, forever responding to texts and emails, almost from the moment our eyes crack open in the morning until our heads hit the pillow at night.

This is the heart that scrunches down into Netflix and football and video games at the first opportunity, as soon as the workday lets up long enough to give us a minute to call our own. This is the heart that looks up from watching YouTube shorts, one after another, and then wonders what just happened with the last two-and-a-half hours.

This is the heart so preoccupied with the demands of growing a business or perfecting a skill that it's lost all sensitivity for focusing on anything that doesn't contribute to its own pursuit of what feels like success. This is the heart deceived into thinking that consuming news and political commentary is more important than any other information we could be gathering at any given moment.

It's a heart overrun with true crime documentaries and cultural podcasts and Amazon purchases and travel ball. A heart that's forgotten what it's like to have an original thought anymore. A heart whose first impulse at the sound of a spare moment is to reach for the smartphone.

And do you know what else it is? It's a heart that's too busy to hear from God. Therefore, it's a heart that produces little if any fruit. Because fruit doesn't grow amid the thorns of distraction.

Fruit only grows in the fertile soil of hearing God's Word, of valuing God's presence.

I can't say it enough. The volume of God's voice, when He speaks to His children, is subtle. It's a whisper. The cadence of His words, as they resonate in our spirits, is imperceptible to the untrained ear. We must discipline ourselves to pick up on His whisper by slowing down, by setting the distractions aside, and by cultivating space for stillness and silence. As one of the mystics has rightly said, "The essential never imposes itself; the unessential is constantly imposing itself."[7] The volume of temporal temptations and distractions is ear-piercing, while the voice of our Father is faint.

Charles Spurgeon, the prince of preachers, was known to have attendees sit silently for a minute at the conclusion of his message, instead of just rushing off to the next item on the order of service. He knew how the Holy Spirit worked in people's lives—not by keeping the schedule rolling but by allowing the seed enough time to set. He understood that his responsibility to his hearers was not merely delivering them information but creating an environment that made possible in them a divine transformation.

The Quakers employed a similar practice, something they termed "expectant waiting." Robert Barclay, a Scottish Quaker living in the 1600s, said, "When assembled, the great work of one and all ought to be to wait upon God, and returning out of their own thoughts and imaginations, to feel the Lord's presence and know a 'gathering into His Name' indeed, where he is 'in the midst' according to His promise."[8]

I've found it beneficial to bring some of these "waiting" techniques into my own times of sitting quietly with the Lord. Because, as I've told you, I need a lot of help in this area. Being as prone to distractions as I am, it is no easy task preparing my heart to receive what He wants to give me today. But I feel like I'm probably in good company. Most all of us need guidance in learning how to rest, to truly rest, in His peace and in His presence.

I usually start by (1) *quieting my body*, positioning myself in a posture where my muscle tension and movement are relaxed, allowing me to breathe slowly and deeply enough until I can feel the effects of it from my toes to my fingertips. Then, (2) *quieting my mind*—releasing what can be handled tomorrow; informing the parts of my brain that do the scheduling, the studying, and the problem-solving that I am ordering them to take a break. Finally, (3) *quieting my critic*, letting go of all the negative judgments and scoldings that I've been firing against myself all day. There's always room for repenting, of course, for cleansing this willful, earthly vessel of the "sin that so easily ensnares" and entangles (Heb. 12:1). I want it filled with nothing but pure thoughts and obedient actions, to the praise of God's grace. But most of the voices in my head do not lead to sanctification or to any lasting change; they only condemn me for sins and for other stupidities that God has already washed in the sea of His forgiveness. They're not helping me become more godly, just more ashamed. And more distracted.

None of these "quieting" practices occur instantaneously: body, mind, and critic. They take a minute. But when I get there, once I'm quiet, I wait.

Yet the distractions keep floating up anyway, interfering with my stillness. "Did I lock the back door?" "What do I want for dinner tonight?" "What was that noise I just heard over there?" It's stunning how actively mindless our overactive minds can be.

That's when I often try to imagine I'm sitting on the shoreline looking out into the ocean as a steady stream of ships pass in front of me, representing the thoughts that are constantly waving at me for my attention. I'm tempted to go join them, to let them take me off to wherever they're going. But I deliberately allow each boat to parade on past without swimming out and climbing in. And with each passing distraction, I utter a simple phrase that brings me back to the task at hand, sitting quietly in the living presence of God.

I'm not talking about a mantra. A shapeless, pointless incantation. Neither am I advocating for chanting words repeatedly. I'm borrowing this practice of a focused word or phrase from Pete Scazzero, longtime pastor and author of the Emotionally Healthy series of books for churches and Christian leaders, and I've seen it work in cutting through my own thorn-choked tangles of distraction.

He once invited a priest to come lead his staff in the practice of silence. Each person was instructed to sit for twenty minutes in the total quiet, and every time their mind wandered, they were to return to the Lord by reciting a biblical word or phrase.

During the season of revival that I've told you about at our church, while I was sitting with the Lord on the porch each night, I selected the phrase "*Abba*, Father" from Romans 8:15: "For you did not receive a spirit of slavery to fall back into fear. Instead, you received the Spirit of adoption, by whom we cry out, '*Abba*, Father!'"

The ships of distracted thoughts would regularly appear, and I would gently and quietly say, either silently or aloud, "*Abba*, Father." Then after a while, the traffic would thin, and I'd be left alone with Him—unbothered, unbattered, head bowed in His presence. To hear Him. To hear *only* Him.

Pete Scazzero shared how, upon completion of this exercise at *their* church, a discouraged member of his staff said, "I think I failed at this. My mind wandered a hundred times in those twenty minutes."

"No," the priest responded. "You didn't fail. Think of it this way: You had a hundred opportunities to return back to God."

We never lose when we seek the Lord, when we choose His presence over our own problems, our own pressures, our own preoccupations. The thing that costs us is all the time we've given over to our demanding distractions, only to come away with nothing. When we could have had everything.

When we could have had *Him.*

You understand, of course, I'm not saying we should check out from handling our day-to-day responsibilities. We all have jobs to do. We all have people depending on us. But staying true to the principles of hard work and personal accountability is not in competition with the practice of living in the presence of God. The problem lies somewhere else.

I think that's what Jesus was saying during His visit to the home of two sisters, Mary and Martha, in Luke 10. Martha tends to get a bad rap for being obsessed with her work, especially for having a martyr's complex about it, though I don't believe Jesus was discounting the work she was doing. Serving others is a worthy endeavor. Welcoming people into our homes, as she did, is part of sharing His grace and goodness with those around us. Hospitality was not what Jesus was trying to stamp out of her life by speaking to her as He did.

The trouble in her heart was distraction. "Martha was distracted by her many tasks" (Luke 10:40), which made her feel offended by Mary's posture of sitting at Jesus's feet and hanging on His every word. The work Martha was doing wasn't the problem; letting it distract her away from Jesus was the problem. Distracted into questioning His loving heart for her—"Lord, don't you care?" Distracted into judging Mary's motives and priorities—"My sister has left me to serve alone." Distracted into thinking she could order Jesus to do something about it—"Tell her to give me a hand" (v. 40). Her words indicated her *life* was out of order, even while she busied herself keeping her house in order.

And so, even if she had gone to sit at His feet with Mary, "listening to what he said" (v. 39), she still would've had a hard time focusing on what Jesus was saying because of all the uproar churning in her mind. She would still have been distracted by all these duties of hers that weren't getting done because she was just sitting there.

Here, then, was the real issue, as diagnosed by the words and wisdom of Jesus: "You are worried and upset about many things" (v. 41). Martha's problem didn't come from having a lot to do; it came from giving those things the power to distract her attention away from the most important thing. For if she could've quieted herself long enough to hear what He was saying, she could've learned not only that dwelling in His presence was the "one thing" that is "necessary" (v. 42), but she could experience the reality of His presence even while accomplishing the necessary business of each ordinary day.

If you don't believe me, believe what was reported about another of those mystics, Brother Lawrence, a French monastic from the 1600s, known to us from his classic work *The Practice of the Presence of God*.

> Even when he was busiest in the kitchen, it was evident that the brother's spirit was dwelling in God. He often did the work that two usually did, but he was never seen to bustle. Rather, he gave each chore the time that it required, always preserving his modest and tranquil air, working neither slowly nor swiftly, dwelling in calmness of soul and unalterable peace.[9]

Before God can do a work *through* us, He must first do a work *on* us and *in* us. Before God brings revival, whether to a church, a family, a group, or an individual, He must first deal with whatever blood clot is preventing revival from flowing freely into our lives. And rarely is this blockage coming from the normal work of the day itself. It comes instead from that hyperactive impulse we've been obeying and cultivating, the one that shows up in our screen time, the one that draws us toward anything that keeps us from having to deal with life's deepest questions, the one that keeps us from maybe ever spending unhurried, undistracted time in His presence.

The devil's most potent weapon of mass destruction is distraction. If we clog the soil of our lives with too much stuff, and if we don't make an effort to clear it of thorns and other invasive species of priorities, we will not be ready—we *can't* be ready—for Him to produce in our hearts the kind of change, the kind of "fruit" that only comes from wanting *Him*, more than we want anything.

So, what about you? Does your activity for God overshadow your time with God? Do you have a hard time being present with God? Do you feel energized in doing things for God and for others, yet you struggle to sit and listen to Him? Do you find it difficult to wait on Him? Do you have a hard time discerning His direction? *Hearing* from Him?

I'm just saying it's all too possible to do ministry for Jesus without having intimacy with Jesus. The noise and distractions will always demand the driver's seat, but the only places they seem capable of taking us are to places where God's voice is the hardest to hear.

Don't let the Martha in you convince you that activity is more important than intimacy. Don't let the urgent needs of the moment continually divert your eyes and ears away from the eternal.

In a world that values productivity over presence, choose presence.

In a culture that rewards busyness over being, choose being.

In a time when everyone is distracted, choose to be fully present with the One who is always present with you.

Don't let the noise of life drown out the voice of God. Choose to sit at the feet of Jesus. Because the choice is yours. And like Mary's choice, it is the one thing necessary, the choice that will not be taken away from you. Or from me.

If every great movement of God begins by not moving—which the Spirit made clear to me on the porch—I'm determined not to move until He moves. And when He's gotten me quiet enough to listen, I'm determined not to be distracted looking somewhere else.

Part 2

LISTENING

Chapter 5

AND THE WORD BECAME FRESH

The Word is the wire along which the voice of God will certainly come to you if the heart is hushed and the attention fixed.[10]

F. B. Meyer

Nothing in my background prepared me for tackling Greek 101 in seminary—"baby Greek," as they call it. I wasn't even very good at English, the one language I knew. How was I supposed to figure out an ancient language I'd never once heard anyone speak before?

But the way you learn everything is the way you learn anything: by putting in the time and practice until you increasingly become proficient at something. I still keep on my bookshelf the original note cards I created two decades ago as a reminder of what it took to start from scratch. And to scratch out an A.

And yet to learn a language, as I'm sure you discovered if you took Spanish or French in school, the cards and the conjugations are only part of the process. Communicating in a language that is not your native tongue requires getting around people who speak it themselves. Interacting with them. Listening to them. Making out the subtle nuance of sounds. Hearing the words on the page come alive in real-world contexts and conversations.

You never become fluent in any language—Italian, German, Japanese, or Russian—until you've immersed yourself in places where it's spoken. Why would communicating with God be any different? Why wouldn't we need to surround ourselves with the language of His kingdom if we ever expect to grasp what the King is saying?

God is always speaking. That's a fact. But here's the question: Are we seeking Him in the places where He most clearly speaks? Especially in the *one* place He speaks, in His Word?

And when He speaks, are we listening?

I want to share with you a simple practice the Holy Spirit used at Long Hollow in getting us listening for Him more regularly through His Word, not realizing God's people had been hearing His voice this way, using this same pattern, for more than 1,500 years.

I've recently picked up a new hobby. I've really gotten into art appreciation, particularly European art from the fifteenth to nineteenth centuries: Caravaggio, Rubens, Michelangelo, da Vinci. For most of my life, I couldn't tell the difference between a Rembrandt and a Renoir, but that's because I hadn't yet made the effort to study and observe their work and distinguish the kinds of craftsmanship that set their pieces apart.

The reason I like art is because it moves you beyond mere words or facts. If you read in the Bible about Jesus calling Matthew to be His disciple, for instance, you import that information into your brain, just as it's written. You believe it in black-and-white. But when you see this biblical fact imagined as Caravaggio did in his 1600 painting *The Calling of Saint Matthew*, you're struck by the shock of disbelief on the tax collector's face and by the shading and color of all the possible storylines the painting captures. It brings the words to life. Pictures give meaning and depth to truth.

The same thing happens when you read or hear a parable of Jesus. Through the vehicle of story, He could take a top-shelf theological concept and make it accessible and memorable to anyone. He could "declare things kept secret from the foundation of the world" (Matt. 13:35) to people who, like us, simply did not have what it took to understand it otherwise.

But parables could only be heard by listeners. That's what made them so incredible. Though all the people in Jesus's audience were hearing the same words spoken, not everyone was getting what He was saying. His parables allowed Him to reveal truth to those who were ready to receive it and yet mask the deeper message He was expressing from those who didn't want to know it anyway.

That's why when I'm talking with my discipleship group about the way Jesus taught, I tell them to draw a line in their Bibles between Matthew 12 and Matthew 13. Up until Matthew 12, He preached openly to the crowds, speaking plainly for all to hear. But by Matthew 13, He'd begun dropping hints, telling the crowds that it was time for them to choose: Was He the Messiah sent from God, or was He not?

So look at this and notice. From Matthew 13 on, He began telegraphing His teaching only to those who were receptive to Him, not to those who rejected Him. He started hiding the truth in parables so that only those who wanted to know Him—"anyone who has ears" (Matt. 13:9)—could hear.

In fact, His first parable was essentially a hearing test. And for our purposes at this point, I think it might be a good idea if we pulled out that story again—the parable of the sower—like we did in the previous chapter, and take our seat in the patient's chair. To see how well we're listening to Him today.

In this story, Jesus illustrated the most integral and beneficial of all the spiritual disciplines: engaging with Him through His Word. The people in His day, of course, had only the Old Testament Scriptures, and most of their exposure to them came not from reading the texts themselves but from hearing them read. Still, God's primary form of communication was, and is, through His Word, through the Bible. That's where we should look first if we say we're serious about wanting to hear from Him. Because His words are already there.

But they still require listening. Listening not just to *them* but to *Him*.

Again, the purpose of this teaching—the parable of the sower—is not to point out why so many people reject Christ in the first place; it's to ascertain why some of those who've already received Christ can't seem to *get* anyplace, why they're not able to hear His voice and obey Him. And all of it has to do with how they, and how we, choose to seek and respond to His Word.

The four soils. You'll remember them.

1. *The path.* One of the adjectives that describes us sometimes is hard-hearted. We're cold toward God and unmoved by His Word. Maybe we're mad at Him. Maybe we've been hurt by the church. Maybe we're locked into a pattern of sin, or we're persisting in harboring bitterness and unforgiveness in our hearts against someone or against the circumstances we've been dealt. But a calloused heart, whatever its cause, is a fire wall to hearing from God through His Word. Nothing gets through when we're not wanting to listen.

2. *The rocks.* Rocky soil is descriptive of those seasons when we're hit-and-miss in our time with Scripture. There's no depth to the experience. We're content living in the shallow end. Even if we were to encounter a rough patch that drove us back to reconnecting with God in His Word, we haven't cultivated anything sustainable in this top layer of soil. So our relationship with Him feels thin and forced at first, like strangers, because we haven't talked with Him in a long time. Getting to know Him in the Bible just hasn't been too important to us.

3. *The thorns.* The crowded soil, like we've already talked about, keeps us pockmarked with distractions. But, as it specifically describes our relationship with Scripture, it becomes sort of a Sunday morning thing. We show up at church, we take notes during the sermon, and we enjoy our interaction with Him in His Word, but by Sunday night we're already off to reality television and fantasy football. We're playing a part where meeting with God is only one of the parts of what we do. And hearing God's voice is not a consistent part of it.

Listening is the seedbed of love. To love someone is to listen to them. That's why we could replace the word *love* with the word *listen* in what Jesus defined as the greatest commandment, and it would still say much the same thing, just in a different way. Imagine Luke 10:27 sounding like this: "*Listen to* the Lord your God with all your heart, with all your soul, with all your strength, and with all your mind, and *listen to* your neighbor as yourself." The slight twist on the well-known wording gives a practical flavor to where our love for God (and for others) begins and what it's meant to entail.

So let me ask you, before we land in the fourth and final type of soil (because there's not much to inspire us about living in these first three kinds)—Why do we persist in not listening? Or, on our best days, half listening? Not just you; I'm talking to me too. What's happened to make us feel okay perpetuating a relationship with God where reading His Word is not much more than a checklist to complete? And where, even when we do read, we don't stop very often to really listen to what He's saying? Or to wonder if maybe we are the reason, not His reluctance, for why we can't seem to find Him sometimes when we want Him?

Another of my hobbies, which I gave up after surrendering to Christ, was being a music DJ. Back in the day, when I was heavy in the party scene, I would invite friends over, hook up a pair of Technic 1200 turntables, and spin vinyl records while everybody hung out.

But during the lull of COVID, I got the itch for making music again. I downloaded a digital program that allowed me to create my own music just by importing sounds into it, in hopes of coming up with new stuff to play while I was doing my workouts at home by myself. And even though I have a rudimentary knowledge of music theory and a viable capability for mixing, I was lost trying to figure out the system, the buttons, the files, the sequencer. Basically, I was ignorant of how to engage with the complicated software. I couldn't get anything out of it.

And I think, when someone says they're not getting anything out of the Bible, the trouble often comes from a similar source. We've downloaded this big program onto our hard drive, and we've read through a lot of its instructions and information. We think everything we should need for the Bible to produce the sound of God's voice in our hearts is discoverable from within our knowledge base. But despite what we do, we don't hear much of anything. Very little of it sounds clear and discernible. We just can't seem to *engage* with it.

That's because engaging with the Bible is less about *data* and more about *da'at*. (What's *da'at*?) *Da'at* is the Hebrew word for "knowing." It's a word you hear most notably perhaps in the early pages of the Bible, where we're told, "Adam knew Eve his wife; and she conceived" (Gen. 4:1 KJV)—meaning, of course, he was intimate with her.

Jesus, when He told His followers they would "know the truth" by continuing in His Word (John 8:32), was referring to this aspect of "knowing"—not just spending time ingesting biblical information but experiencing through it the intimacy of a personal relationship with God.

If the only thing His disciples needed from Him was an infusion of knowledge, He would've just placed His hands on their heads and instantly transmitted what they needed to know. Instead, He told them to "know the truth" the same way we develop a close relationship with someone—through being with them, communing with them, enjoying fellowship with them. That's what our time in the Bible is intended to be and accomplish. To spend time in it is to invest in the ongoing process of developing a relationship with Him—with *Him* and His truth, with *Him* through His Word.

That's what the rest of the people who heard Him teach didn't understand, even the ones who'd devoted their lives to parsing and interpreting the law and the prophets as the centerpiece of their religious devotion. "You pore over the Scriptures," Jesus said, "because you think you have eternal life in them, and yet they testify about me. But you are not willing to come to me"—to experience, through His Word, a true relationship with God—"so that you may have life" (John 5:39–40).

The Bible is a book, yes, but to open it is to be invited into a relationship with the living God. He doesn't just want to be read about. He wants to be known, to be worshipped, to be enjoyed, to be heard. And for this, we need hearts composed of "good" soil.

Not the path.

Not the rocks.

Not the thorns.

4. *The good ground.* Softened and tilled up. Cleared of needless distraction. Made receptive to nourishment and to the growth of the seed. Able to yield exponential levels of fruitfulness by the work of the Holy Spirit quickening the truth in our hearts—"some a hundred, some sixty, some thirty times what was sown" (Matt. 13:23). These are the times, under these soil conditions, when we can expect God's Word to come alive for us, to become fresh words for us.

When we're receptive to Him.

Seeking intimacy with Him.

When we're listening.

Many of us, knowing the value of being consistent in the Scripture, will often commit ourselves to a systematic plan of Bible reading. And that's great. I'm all in favor of being disciplined about staying regularly in the Word. I do it myself. We should all do it.

But sometimes, chunking through several chapters of Scripture a day can start to feel like more of the goal than growing this relationship with God we've been talking about, as if He is more pleased by the volume of our intake than by our desire for meeting with Him. Again, I'm not dictating one solitary way for interacting with the Bible. Reading through it in a year is an accomplishment. I'm just suggesting that we're not out to break distance records, and certainly not to feel spiritually superior to others because of our quiet-time achievements. We are here, more than anything, to hear from Him.

And I've found I hear Him best in Scripture when I am *meditating* on His Word.

Meditation is slow. It incorporates a lot of the qualities of silence and stillness and solitude that we talked about in the first section. Benedict, the sixth-century monk who put together one of the first known manuals for monks and monasteries, considered the first rule of spiritual life to be *obsculta*, the idea of listening attentively. He believed God's Word was meant to be absorbed through sitting in contemplation, in meditation. Not just listening with one's ears but "with the ear of your heart," he said.[11]

The first mention of meditation in the Bible is found when Isaac, waiting for his bride Rebekah to arrive, "went out to meditate in the field toward evening" (Gen. 24:63 ESV). The Hebrew word that's used for "meditate" here is *suach*, which can be translated as *contemplating* or *considering* or *communing* with oneself or with God. Another word that commonly translates as "meditate" is *hagah*, which means "to reflect, to rehearse, to whisper, to coo like a dove," or (my favorite) "to chew like a cow."

We once raised two Scottish Highland cows on our property: Corrie (after Corrie ten Boom) and Fred (just because). I eventually got rid of both of them after they'd kicked me a few too many times. But while they were here, I'm not sure I ever saw these animals when they were not chewing the cud. And it always served to remind me of this principle of meditation.

Since cows are usually breaking down tough plant material through their digestive system, they often bring it back up into their mouths so they can continue to chew on it—to ruminate on it—to maximize the levels of nutrients their bodies can absorb from it. And when we meditate on Scripture, we are doing something similar. We are chewing on God's Word, both mentally and spiritually, allowing its deeper truths to work their way through us.

Benedict's name for this practice was the *Lectio Divina*, Latin for "divine reading." And, sort of like the four stomachs of a cow, it includes four movements that guide its participants through the process of meditating slowly on the Scripture, slowly enough to hear from God.

I'll share them with you here. Imagine yourself applying them wherever you are.

1. *Lectio (or reading).* In this opening part, you read whatever portion of Scripture you're reading, but instead of just trying to get through it, you focus on listening attentively, listening for any words or phrases that particularly catch your notice.

2. *Meditatio (or meditation).* Chew individually on those various pieces that stuck out to you as you were reading. Repeat them aloud or internally, and allow the Holy Spirit to connect these biblical truths with any emotions or memories of yours, any questions or life situations that are currently top-of-mind for you.

3. *Oratio (or prayer).* Having mulled it over in your own thoughts, take time now to dialogue with God about what you've been pondering. Depending on what you're contemplating, form your prayer into a confession, or a request, or a song of praise, or whatever it draws out of you. In doing so, you're moving that biblical word or phrase from the intellectual to the practical.

4. *Contemplatio (or contemplation).* Finally, rest in God's presence as you sit quietly and digest what you've learned from this experience—what you've learned about truth, what you've learned about Him. Some people refer to this step as "wasting time with God," which quite often grates against the setting on our inner clock. But don't be in a rush to move on from being in His presence. Remember, that's what you're here for. To deepen your relationship with Him. To make your soil receptive to Him. To listen for Him and be changed by Him.

I tell you, I'd never heard of this ancient method for interacting with Scripture until I started doing the reading and research that helped drive what I did on the porch. But as soon as I heard of it, I was blown away by how closely it corresponded with the

H.E.A.R. Journal concept that I'd developed more than ten years earlier.

H.E.A.R.

- Highlight
- Explain
- Apply
- Respond

I'd long used this simple structure to help discipleship groups interact with Scripture on an ongoing basis. I'd seen it assist all kinds of believers in engaging more personally and steadily and effectively with the Word. And after marrying it with the subtle differences from the *Lectio Divina*, and then experiencing personal revival myself by using it in my Bible reading, I couldn't help praising God for bringing it into our church's culture, nearly from the outset of my ministry there.*

Because even though my first years at Long Hollow had been disappointing and discouraging in a lot of ways—both from lots of my mistakes and from a whole lot of spiritual warfare—God had still been faithful to get a lot of us adopting the frequent practice of meditating deeply on His Word. And despite the difficulties that wormed their way into some of our dynamics as a church and as a people, I now believe this focus on *listening*—on *H.E.A.R.ing* from God in His Word—had prepared the soil of our hearts for experiencing revival, just the way He sent it to us.

Historians tell us the people who heard Jesus in the first century were largely illiterate. Fewer than 15 percent of them could read or write. But they could listen. And Jesus filled their ears with stories that revealed His Word to them. Whether in hearing Him teach or in hearing the Scriptures read, they could

* See Appendix 3 for more details about the H.E.A.R. method and journal.

cultivate the kinds of hearts that were eager to receive what God was saying.

Today, in the developed world, literacy is mostly a given. Just about everybody can read and write. Our problem is not *access* to the Word but *ambivalence* to it. Not too many in the modern church are eagerly listening for God's voice. They're not latching onto His every word. Churches are filled with literate believers who are illiterate to their Bible, who don't really care to open it. But no one can claim God never speaks to them while their Bibles lay closed around the house. God speaks through His Spirit in various ways but none so vivid as through the Word He has already given us, the Word He continually breathes through and makes relevant to us.

So, in this situation where we find ourselves today, with voices competing for our attention all over the place, we have a choice to make.

Will we seek to hear the voice of the One who created us, who knows us completely, and who loves us unconditionally, as He consistently says in His Word? Or will we seek out the voices of a culture that changes its mind with every generation?

Will we trust the voice of the One who can see the whole picture when our vision is clouded? Or will we continue to be limited to the perspective of our own best guesses?

Will we cling to the Word of Him who has guided people safely home across the ages, through challenges as dark and dangerous as anything we're experiencing today? Or will we waste our time listening to voices that promise freedom but deliver bondage?

His Word is right here. Hand delivered to us. Readily available to us. Simply awaiting our willingness to immerse ourselves in it and, by doing so, to find a new depth of experience with Him. A new depth of relationship with God. With the God who speaks.

Darrin Patrick was a pastor and author who became a friend after going through a devastating season of losing his way and his church position, only to live out the evidence of true repentance and to walk out the recovery that few are humble enough to experience. He was scheduled to speak at our church one weekend in May, not long after I'd gone out to the porch in desperation myself. I heard from him on Wednesday of that week. On Friday, he tragically took his own life.

Unlike most, Darrin was someone who spoke authentically and vulnerably about himself. He was not afraid of facing his own harsh regrets or of using them as shared warnings to others. And once, during a staff retreat he did with us, where he talked openly about the circumstances that led to the losses he faced, he pinpointed one particular culprit that precipitated his slow fade. "The Bible became for me a tool to use," he told us, "and not a treasure to behold."

Try to imagine a world with no Bible to guide us. Try to imagine how much harder our already hard lives would be if the language of Scripture was not tucked into the folds of our brain and in the impulses of our heart. Try to imagine how desperate we'd be for a way to hear God's voice in language we could understand if it was nowhere to be found. And yet here it is. Not just in the Greek and Hebrew of ancient peoples but in the familiar words and phrases that, by His grace and by design, are able to bring us closer into relationship with the One who speaks them.

Never may the Bible be a mere book on our bookstand, a mere tool in our Christian toolbox. Are we treasuring it, beholding it, even stopping long enough to listen to what God wants to say to us through the knowing language of His Word? To ponder it? To chew on it? Those are good questions to think about.

And, next question, the better question, the one we'll be taking with us into the next chapter: Are we obeying what we hear?

Chapter 6

IF YOU KNOW WHAT'S GOOD FOR YOU

Worship begins in holy expectancy; it ends in holy obedience.[12]

Richard Foster

When God began moving at Long Hollow, I started scouring the writings of other pastors from earlier days who knew how to sustain and encourage revival: Vance Havner, Ron Dunn, Peter Lord, Jack Taylor. All these men were cut from the same cloth. They sought the Lord, and they lived by faith, and they were not afraid to step out and attempt the impossible if God told them to do it.

One of these who impacted me more than the others was Manley Beasley, a powerful evangelist of the twentieth century. I've since listened to more of his sermons than I can count, and I believe I've read every one of his books.

Years ago, I had the privilege of meeting his son Jonathan, who was on staff at a church where I was preaching one Sunday, and later began a friendship with Jonathan's older brother, Manley Jr., as well. From each of them I heard the story of how when their father was needing direction from the Lord, he would tell his wife, Marthé, "Honey, I've got a water jug and my Bible. I'm heading to the woods."

"When will you come back?" she'd ask him.

"When I get a word from God."

That's how confidently he expected God to speak to him and guide him, and I'm convinced we can expect the same. If we'll get quiet before Him (chapter 3), if we'll drastically eliminate our distractions (chapter 4), and if we'll open His Word not just to read it but to meditate on it, to listen for how He speaks through it, and to deepen our intimacy of relationship in it (chapter 5), we, too, can head out with our Bible and our water jug and count on God being there to meet us.

Oh, and one other thing that invites the voice of God: if He knows we'll do what He tells us to do. If He knows we'll *obey* Him.

I think I'd always known and noticed this connection before—the direct line between God's speaking to us and our obedience to Him—but it became front and center for me on the porch, and it has stayed that way ever since. If I'm not feeling spiritually receptive today, it probably has something to do with my hesitancy to obey Him. Because when I am serious about responding quickly to what I perceive to be God's direction, I tend to experience moments of spiritual clarity from Him much more often. So here's what I always tell people: *The duration of time between when God speaks to you and when you respond to Him increases the frequency of His speaking.* The promptness of your obedience increases God's voice in your life.

And then it's like wildfire. It grows on itself. It fuels its own momentum. As I became increasingly fearless and submissive in letting the Holy Spirit directly inspire my sermons, and then I'd go into that auditorium to deliver them, it was as though the floor beneath where people were sitting was several inches deep in kerosene, and all I did was toss out the match. The Word caught fire, and people were drawn toward the flame.

After witnessing that kind of power—knowing it had nothing, seriously nothing to do with me—it fed my hunger to go sit and listen for Him even more. I couldn't wait to get back there, to get back to the porch, not knowing what He would say to me next.

But I knew one thing: I was finally starting to know Him.

"Knowing." The *knowledge* of God we need isn't confined to the classical Greek pursuit of human reason and rationale. Nor is it the conjuring of some kind of secret knowledge from New Age spiritual practices. Knowing God comes from experiencing truth in action as we experience relationship with Him—a knowledge we continually grow into and understand from our day-to-day interaction with Him.

And how do we know it's happening? How do we know we're "knowing" Him?

> This is how we know that we know him: if we keep his commands. (1 John 2:3)

If we obey Him.

It's so clear. It's just that it's maybe not what we want to hear. We don't want our pattern of receiving divine guidance to be so directly tied to our pattern of actions. But obedience is how we experience knowing Him. Obedience fosters intimacy with Him. Obedience doesn't save us; nothing saves but the blood of Christ, of course, the actions of His grace. But the love that flows from us as believers—in our listening, our serving, our humility, in every choice of obedience—that's how we truly come to know Him. "Everyone who loves has been born of God and knows God," John said, but "the one who does not love does not know God" (1 John 4:7–8). The way we know if our love for Him is real, and if our love for others is real, and if our desire for hearing Him is real, is if we're obeying Him for real. Could it be any plainer than that?

That's why, when Jesus was giving final instructions to His followers about going out and making disciples, He told them to start by teaching people "to observe [to obey] everything I have commanded you" (Matt. 28:20). Disciples are made not by how well we teach them Bible information or by how well they take notes on it. Disciples are made by our teaching them and modeling for them *obedience* to Him, knowing we ourselves never outgrow our own need for being obedient followers of Him as well.

Not if we want to keep hearing His voice.

During my intensive time of listening on the porch, one new discipline I discovered became for me then, and continues to be for me now, the most transformative of all.

It's called the *Examen*.

The practice originally began with Ignatius of Loyola (not to be confused with Ignatius of Antioch, one of the earliest Christian martyrs who lived and died within a century of Christ's ministry on earth). The Ignatius I'm talking about was a Spanish nobleman from the 1500s who rethought his feelings about God after being seriously injured in battle and reading the accounts of Dominic and Francis during his recovery. In time, he became founder of the Society of Jesus, known today as the Jesuits, a religious order that took vows of poverty and chastity and, most of all, obedience to the teachings of Christ.

"If you practice no other discipline," Ignatius taught his little band of brothers, "do this one only"—the *Examen*—an examination of our conscience that provides a regular, sustained opportunity for the Holy Spirit to counsel us in the direction of obedience.

Yes, the Holy Spirit.

One of the issues God challenged me to repent about while we were experiencing those days of revival at Long Hollow was that I knew more about Jesus, who was here for thirty years, than the Holy Spirit, who has indwelt believers now for two thousand years.

In the circles I was trained in, we were cautioned to be careful around the Holy Spirit. We were made aware of the many abuses associated with those who claimed to be acting under His influence. And the general impression I took away from how we were taught on the subject said if we knew what was good for us, we'd be better off avoiding the Holy Spirit than inviting Him any closer. Just to be on the safe side.

Only problem is, that's not how Jesus taught His *own* disciples. Sure, He instructed them in the importance of obedience, of course, which I knew about—"If you love me, you will keep my commands" (John 14:15)—but He equally stressed the importance of the coming Holy Spirit, whom I'm ashamed to say I knew little about. "I will ask the Father," He said,

> and he will give you another Counselor to be with you forever. He is the Spirit of truth. The world is unable to receive him because it doesn't see him or know him. But you do know him, because he remains with you and will be in you. (vv. 16–17)

Notice the word *another* in that phrase that says, "another Counselor to be with you." Two different Greek words can be translated "another"—*heteros*, meaning another of a different kind, or the word used here—*allos*—which means another of the same kind. The Holy Spirit is *allos*—the same kind as Jesus. Of the same essence. Of the same substance. Not a ghostly stranger that we should want to distance ourselves from. The Spirit is a member of the Godhead, like the Father, like the Son, whom we should want as near to us as possible.

Imagine if Jesus came back in the flesh again. People would book flights from all over the world to stand in line for the chance to talk with Him. They'd wait for months to get so much as a glimpse of Him, just to be in the proximity of His presence. And yet if we've received Christ as Savior, the Holy Spirit is as present in our lives today as if Jesus were standing right here in front of us.

I do want to hear from the Holy Spirit.

And it happens for me in the *Examen*.

Ignatius encouraged the Jesuits to practice it twice daily—at noon and at end of day. I try to work through it as daily as possible but at least once a week. It's based on two central concepts that help us discern the handiwork of God in our lives: (1) *consolations* and (2) *desolations*. Like our two eyes, these two different types of reflections work together, giving us the most accurate perception of what's happening not only around us but, more importantly, inside us. As you and I think back over our day, or the last week, or the last few weeks, or the last month, or whatever, these consolations and desolations keep before us the specific ways we've either drawn the Spirit closer to us or have pushed Him away and stunted the growth of His fruit in our lives.

And if you don't think the Holy Spirit wants to speak to you about that, just wait.

I usually start with *consolations*—because they're easier—but also because, for most of us, the voice that's chattering inside our heads all day is usually beating us up about something. We need consoling! And by processing through some of the following types of questions, I find I can quiet my inner subcommittee's voice for a while and invite the Holy Spirit, the Comforter, to encourage me in those areas where I've genuinely been letting Him do His thing in me.

- How was I inspired to worship God today?
- How did I demonstrate the fruit of the Spirit? (See Gal. 5:22–23.)
- How did I let Him keep me at peace, even amid challenges?
- How did I let a past sorrow inspire compassion for someone?
- How did I let a past regret lead to a positive change?
- How did I exemplify love to my neighbor?
- How did I sense God's presence with me?
- How was I drawn closer to Him today?
- How did I share Christ with someone?
- How did I let the Spirit lead me?

There's nothing magical about asking this specific set of questions, nor is it an exhaustive list. But I'm sure you get the idea of the kinds of things you might ask alongside the Holy Spirit—things He wants you to see and celebrate together with Him, things He wants to help you build on during the coming days. These findings are encouraging to you not because you've proven something to Him about what you can do when you're on your best behavior. They prove instead what's possible when you—and when I, people who've been as self-driven as we've been—stay open to letting Him be the driver behind what we think and do.

He loves enabling you to be a better father, husband, wife, mother, leader, worker, pastor, or communicator than you or I could ever be. I've tried being all these things (except for a wife or mother, of course) in my own strength, answering to my own voice, and I refuse to go back to those days. Because when the Spirit speaks through me, the message is always more impactful. When He gives me wisdom for leading my family or my staff, His counsel is always better than mine would've been. Every moment of every day, if I'm providing Him room to direct me and speak truth to me—and if I'm determined to obey what He says to me—it'll draw me closer to Him. It'll increase my faith, hope, and joy. It'll help me extend His encouragement to others. And it'll enable me to experience living at settled peace with God.

It'll enliven my relationship with the third member of the Trinity.

As do the *desolations*.

In fact, I'll tell you, this is where the Holy Spirit has performed the deepest work in my life. Just warning you now before we go any further: Prepare yourself for a heart change. In working through some of the following questions pretty regularly, at a consistent pace, I don't think I can adequately remember the number of people I've had to go to and tell them I was sorry. Over the last few years, the inscription on the side of my spiritual bus may as well have read "The Apology Tour."

The Holy Spirit, you know, sees and hears everything, and—if we're listening to Him—He will bring to mind our most imperceptible actions and attitudes, things we habitually tend to gloss over and not want to think about.

- Was I discouraged today?
- Did I feel isolated, alone, unloved?
- Was I stuck in negative thought patterns? How? Why?
- Did I demonstrate the fruit of the flesh? (See Gal. 5:19–21.)
- Was I selfish, prideful, arrogant?
- Was I lethargic, ambivalent, lacking motivation?
- Did I let my sorrows blind me to the needs of others?
- Did I allow my regrets to discount who I am in Christ?
- Did I miss an opportunity to share Christ with someone?
- Did I say something I need to ask forgiveness for?
- Did I quench the Holy Spirit? Did I grieve Him?
- Did I lack wisdom and a sense of direction?
- In what ways was I spiritually dry?
- How was I drawn away from God?

Let's be honest, you and I will never get through a day, much less a week or a month, without producing some lousy answers to questions like these. We've denied God's power, diminishing what we believe He can do. We've dimmed our awareness of His indwelling presence. We've disconnected from Him, directing our attention to other things, convinced they can fill us so much better, so much quicker than the Spirit can.

And it feels bad, hearing Him pinpoint these failures and agitations of ours, these cold areas of darkness in our heart. In fact, I often write down in my journal the ways my answers to these questions make me feel. But in feeling all these things now—on the *back* end—my goal is to let them fine-tune how I listen for the wooing and warning of the Spirit's voice next time on the *front* end. Amid the temptation. Amid the trial. Amid those times when I've so often been oblivious and unfeeling toward Him, both in the past and in the present.

The point of this revealing exercise is not to berate us. It's meant to open our eyes, to reveal our blind spots, to uncover the sins that hide below the surface. And it's meant to open our ears, realizing the same Spirit who reveals to us our brokenness also desires to restore to us our first love by leading us back to Him, by helping us recover with Him. It's all designed to cleanse us, to sanctify us through surrender, so that we can experience the abundant life we've been chasing away every day by chasing the deceits of selfishness, entitlement, and distraction.

When you and I are not afraid to be found out, to be *examined* by the Holy Spirit within us, we become participants with Him in a supernatural process in which He speaks and we respond. In which we start again in obedience. And if we need to repent, we make changes. And if we need to apologize, we make phone calls. And if we've listened to Him well, we make our final answer to Him a prayer of thanks for how He's working in our life. That's how I always finish each journey I take through the *Examen*. By thanking Him.

Thanking Him for all He does for me and all He says to me to help me obey Him.

Once, after I'd spoken to a group of church planters about my time alone with the Lord on the porch, a pastor approached me to inquire about a specific line I'd mentioned in my sermon that day. "You said you 'tuned your ear to hear the accent of the Holy Spirit.' Are you saying God spoke to you outside the Bible?"

I understood exactly where he was coming from. And, honestly, at one point in my life, I'd have probably been just as skeptical of somebody who claimed to hear from God the way I was proposing. But after the ten months I'd spent listening for the Spirit's voice in the quiet, and after the revival we'd continued to experience from our listening for Him, I'd started to widen the wonder of my spiritual mindset.

"God speaks to us in many different ways," I said to him. "The primary way is through His Word, of course, which is always the baseline we use for measuring anything else we think we're hearing from the Lord. But wouldn't you agree God also speaks through other people, through circumstances, through closed doors, through checks in our spirit, things like that?"

"Sure," he said, "but you talk as if you're hearing from heaven directly."

You may not know it to look at me, but I really am sensitive about coming on too strong with people. And I try hard not to do it, unless I feel the situation calls for it. Because, listen, no way am I saying I have a private line to heaven that others cannot access. I am not the least bit more popular with God than any other believer. But something fearless rises up within you after, like Manley Beasley, you've gotten a word from God. You don't fear men anymore; you only fear not being obedient to what He's told you.

I'm talking about the *rhema* word from God. The New Testament uses two words for "word"—*logos*, meaning the revelation of God that's found in Scripture; and *rhema*, meaning the spoken word. Think of it as the Word of God (the Bible) applied to your life in a particular situation. You never need to wonder whether the Holy Spirit will contradict the written Word since, after all, He inspired every word of it (see 2 Pet. 1:21). But His role for us today is to take the *logos* Word and apply it to specific areas of our lives through a *rhema* word. Inspiration plus application equals transformation.

That's why Paul, in telling us to take up "the sword of the Spirit—which is the word of God" (Eph. 6:17), didn't use the word *logos* there but *rhema*. What we need from the Spirit is the Word of God delivered to us with razor-sharp direction on how to live this Word in our daily lives, so we can apply it and obey it and feel our relationship with Him coming to life "through the word of Christ" (Rom. 10:17 ESV). Again, it's the *rhema* word there in this verse from Romans—Paul's choice of words, not mine—working together with the *logos* Word in our lives to help animate "faith" within us. How cool is that!

So when this gentleman came up to me, implying I was stirring up trouble by talking about listening for the Holy Spirit's voice in my normal comings and goings as a Christian, I felt released to frame my answer in blunt language: "Brother, I don't mean to be offensive, but when was the last time you spent ten months in silence and solitude for two hours every night, bending your ear to hear from God?" A better question for most of us—including me too, for the longest time—would've asked how long it's been since we spent ten *days*, ten *hours*, maybe even just ten *minutes* listening for the Holy Spirit to sculpt our plans with His sword.

All I know is, if we did, we'd hear a lot more from Him.

And if we obeyed what He said, we'd hear even more.

I just go back to that week leading up to what became the ninety-nine-person Sunday that kicked off our experience of revival at Long Hollow. "Spontaneous baptisms" was the word I kept hearing on the porch. I knew it had biblical precedent from Peter's message at Pentecost: "Repent and be baptized," he said, "each of you" (Acts 2:38)—all those who'd been "pierced to the heart" (v. 37) by hearing the gospel so vividly explained by the preacher and demonstrated in the coming of the Holy Spirit. Yet with the other side of my brain, I could just as easily have ruled the whole thing out. *Does that mean it's for US? What should I do? Listen? Or let it go?*

God taught me so much about the Spirit during that season of renewal He gave us. He taught me, for example, that you can't manufacture revival. You can't just shake up the song selection or craft a slicker sermon series or change the order of service to try igniting it. He also taught me, primarily through my friend Michael Catt, that the pastor's job during revival is to be a "tender of the fire"—sometimes stacking the wood to keep it going, sometimes using a poker to move the coals around, sometimes just letting the heat simmer, at other times being willing to let the fire go out, to discern when the season is closing. But although you can't really plan for revival and you certainly should never seek to manipulate it, you do need to be obedient to whatever the

Spirit is starting to say to your listening ears. God may not lead you to do spontaneous baptisms, as He did with us. You may not even believe you feel doctrinally cleared for doing it. That's okay. But you do need to be open to hearing the voice of God. And you need to do whatever He tells you.

You can only say two things about everything in life: "I wish I had" or "I'm glad I did." And I do not want to die saying the first. Do you?

So take your Bible, take your water jug, and prepare to hear something from the Spirit in the stillness that'll free you forever from peddling in sidebar conversations and frivolous activities. You won't quibble anymore over whether He speaks to His people or not, and you won't fear going forward on it once you've heard Him speak to you. You'll be too busy doing it, learning why *living* the Bible is even better than *knowing* the Bible. And why listening and obeying can never keep from living side by side together. Smiling ear to ear.

Part 3

RHYTHM

Chapter 7

THE $86,400 QUESTION

The choice before us today is what it always was—whether to be worldly or unworldly, whether to live for the unloving self or to live for the love of God.[13]

Joy Davidman

In 1367, five hundred years before Big Ben, but on the same site as the now famous bell and its iconic tower overlooking Parliament, England's first public chiming clock struck the hour in London. Within a century, similar clocks would become commonplace in city centers throughout Europe. Thus began the subtle transition away from using natural light as the primary means of telling time, moving instead toward the metallic drumbeat of the man-made clock.

In 1879, with Thomas Edison's invention of the incandescent light bulb, a similar shifting took place beneath the human experience. No longer was nighttime a natural winding down of the day. Whereas the typical American of the late 1800s was accustomed to sleeping as many as ten hours a night on average, future generations could now push back the arrival of darkness by flooding it with artificial light, creating an endless environment for after-hours activity.

Then in 2007, the iPhone. Hard to believe, isn't it, that a creation so permanently attached to our hip didn't even exist as recently as twenty years ago. The normal user engages with his or her smartphone two-and-a-half hours every day—minimum—picking it up seventy or eighty or a hundred times a day, starting usually before they've gotten out of bed. Leaving home without it is like forgetting where you left your child. Even if you're already miles down the road, even if it makes you embarrassingly late getting to where you're going, you'll still turn around and head back for it. Better than having to spend the whole day separated from a device you don't know how to live without anymore.

The point is this: *Something* will dictate the rhythm of your life. It may be the pressure of the clock; it may be the ten things needing to get done before you go to bed tonight; it may be whatever electronic impulse pulls you back toward your cell phone for the hundredth time today. But depending on what is dictating your rhythm, you'll either be open to hearing the voice of God, or you'll be so connected to other things that your only connection with Him is reduced to passing Him in the hallway, on your way to wherever you think you're supposed to go next.

But what if, instead of letting the clock determine your rhythm, instead of letting your do-list determine your rhythm, instead of letting your iPhone determine your rhythm, *you* determined your rhythm.

It could make the difference of a lifetime.

The Lord created the world to operate in rhythm. The sun and moon cycle through the sky each day at set rhythms. The seasons come and go and come again according to an established rhythm. The ocean tides both surge and recede at a precise, predictable rhythm. Even amid a world at chaos, the whole thing rides on an ancient foundation of rhythm.

If we stop to notice, we'll even feel the rhythm inside ourselves. Our bodies follow what's called a circadian rhythm—the physical, mental, and behavioral changes that mark the way we experience each twenty-four-hour period. Our hearts beat to a rhythm. Our breathing occurs at a rhythm. All the systems at work inside us, most of them moving involuntarily without any effort of will on our part, continue plodding away at this invisible rhythm.

We'll talk before long about Sabbath, another sense of rhythm that's built into us by God as His created people. But the fact that we don't see these rhythms unless we're looking for them, and that we don't hear them unless we're listening for them, doesn't mean they don't exist. It just means we've become more accustomed to living at a *different* rhythm.

You remember, of course, in the final moments before Jesus was betrayed, how He took His three closest disciples deep into the garden. He left them to stand watch with Him, to be present with Him, to pray for Him while He withdrew to an even more secluded spot a short distance away.

Three times He returned, and three times He found them sleeping. And with what we know now about what Jesus was facing, and about the agonizing prayers He was offering alone to His Father just beyond where these three friends were stretched out asleep, could any question cut more deeply into a believer's heart than the one He asked of Peter: "Couldn't you stay awake with me one hour?" (Matt. 26:40).

Just *one* hour?

Notice that Jesus didn't ask this question of the other two. He singled Peter out. Maybe that's because, more than the others, Jesus wanted Peter to have these words in mind when, three times before this night was over, he would deny having any kind of relationship with Jesus at all. I think it's fair to say if Peter had stayed awake in the garden—if he'd been in rhythm with Jesus for even that one hour—he might not have failed Him so miserably in the courtyard. His attention to each hour, to the importance of each hour, to the rich opportunities for communing with God that reside within each hour, might've prevented him from being so unprepared for those next few harrowing hours.

And I wonder how many of our own failures, our own missteps, our own stumbling around and falling in trying to follow Christ, could be traced back to all those single hours we missed?

The hours we spent sleepwalking. Whole hours we didn't even notice as they passed by. Hours we could've spent attuned to God's presence. But we were so accustomed to spending them on everything else. We were so engrained at dancing to a different rhythm—to our own rhythm, to others' rhythms, and to all the chiming-clock rhythms of the world—when we were made to move at *God's* rhythm.

If you're looking for a definable rhythm in Scripture, you'll find it most often in the measure of a single day.

> Give us today our daily bread. (Matt. 6:11)
>
> Encourage each other daily, while it is still called today. (Heb. 3:13)
>
> [Jesus] said to them all, "If anyone wants to follow after me, let him deny himself, take up his cross daily, and follow me." (Luke 9:23)
>
> Even though our outer person is being destroyed, our inner person is being renewed day by day. (2 Cor. 4:16)

Dailiness creates an environment for hearing from God. He established this rhythm right from the beginning in the daily cadence of creation. But no sooner had He rescued the Old Testament people of Israel from slavery in Egypt than He immediately established with them another daily rhythm as they journeyed toward the promised land.

> The LORD said to Moses, "I am going to rain bread from heaven for you. The people are to go out each day and gather enough for that day. This way I will test them to see whether or not they will follow my instructions." (Exod. 16:4)

In the rain, in the heat, in the wind, every day, they were required to go out and bring in their daily allotment of manna. When they were sick, when they were tired, when it was the last thing they felt like doing, each day called for that day's work, except on the Sabbath, when God provided for two days.

In the manna He was offering them life. Through His provision in the wilderness, He was offering them a future. But to experience it, to go forward with Him, they needed to keep an immovable appointment with Him.

Today.

On its face, the little bit of manna they gleaned from each day's harvest didn't amount to much. Just enough for that day's needs. There wasn't any saving it for tomorrow. If they tried hoarding it away and building up a surplus, it grew worms and turned rancid. The secret wasn't in the manna; the secret was in daily obedience. In *dailiness.* God was teaching them through this daily chore the discipline of depending on Him. Of maintaining a daily relationship with Him. And every day for forty years, they would learn it again each morning.

We, too, must learn it again each day ourselves. The Lord had to teach it to me again on the porch—slowly but surely, night after night. Dailiness is the operating system that supports our spiritual life. Just as we can't delegate our devotional time with God to someone else, having them do it for us, neither can we delegate today's moments with God to tomorrow. By staying fully engaged in the present and in the parameters of each day, we marry the essential quality of stillness with the mighty power of patience. We allow ourselves to wait on Him because . . . because we've got all day. And because, really, we have nothing else. But because we do have today, we have all the required materials for hearing the One who's told us not to "worry about tomorrow" (Matt. 6:34).

So let's think back to the clock. And to our never-ending list of uncompleted chores and ambitions. And to the texts and emails and ball scores and social media posts that chime in on our day from morning to evening and sometimes deep into the night. You know the rhythm of *that* lifestyle. Lots of pressure. Lots of people's high demands. Lots of frustration and burnout and doubting ourselves, discouraged by the speed with which we're accomplishing life. Lots of entertaining wastes of time that leave behind nothing but junk-food wrappers crowding our empty minds.

Consider instead a different kind of day. A different kind of *rhythm* to your day.

I found it in what's known as the Divine Office, another monastic practice first instituted by Benedict in the sixth century but maintained throughout history and still common today even among the modern laity. Sometimes called Fixed-Hour Prayer or the Liturgy of the Hours, the Divine Office (from the Latin for "work") differs from a normal quiet time in that it's not an extended once-a-day meeting with God in His Word and in prayer but an all-day pattern of reflecting on Him.

The Bible is filled with examples of people who practiced something similar. "Evening, and morning, and at noon, will I pray," David shared in the words of Psalm 55:17 (KJV). The writer of Psalm 119 spoke, too, of how "I praise you seven times a day for your righteous judgments" (v. 164). Daniel, we know, prayed "three times a day," giving "thanks to his God" from a room in his house (Dan. 6:10). And it doesn't stop there. "Devout Jews in Jesus' time prayed two to three times a day," writes author and pastor Pete Scazzero. "Jesus himself probably followed the Jewish custom of praying at set times during the day. After Jesus' resurrection, his disciples continued to pray at certain hours of the day (Acts 3:1; 10:9)."[14]

Shortly after becoming a believer, I spent a weekend at the Saint Joseph Abbey Monastery in Covington, Louisiana, where I marveled at the monks following this practice, which divides the day into eight appointments with God:

1. *Vigils/Matins:* middle of the night (normally 3:45 a.m.)

2. *Lauds:* early morning (6:00 a.m.)
3. *Prime:* first sign of daylight (6:45 a.m.)
4. *Terce:* midmorning (9:00 a.m.)
5. *Sext:* noon (12:00 p.m.)
6. *None:* mid-afternoon (2:00 p.m.)
7. *Vespers:* evening (5:45 p.m.)
8. *Compline:* night (7:45 p.m.)

Look at all these sacred spaces made available to us by the simple passing of each ordinary day, opportunities to stop for just a moment—those moments when otherwise we'd probably be reaching for our phones—just to acknowledge the rule and reality of God in the midst of whatever we're doing.

Now perhaps you see this list and think, *No way, I can't keep up with that.* But the iPhone, again, is just the perfect example that says you surely can. I dare you one day to look and see how many pickups you've logged, where you've reached for your phone at your desk or from your pocket or in the few seconds before a traffic light turns green. If you do it double-digits or less each day, you're in the minority. Standard usage patterns would put you at 100 or more. Looking for what? A headline? A Dow Jones report? Another stroll through everybody's socials? A check of text messages, as if none of them can wait? So, yes, you stop and observe the gospel according to smartphone so often that it's hard for you to put it down, where every click leads to another one, to the tap of the next app in your usual rotation. But to acknowledge God for a moment or two in prayer, with a word of praise, with a recognition of thanks, is just too much to ask?

If you search, you can find all kinds of guides detailing the way many people observe the daily schedule of the Divine Office with selected readings and hymns and recited prayers and other things. But please don't get hung up on the method. As far as I'm concerned, the choices you or I make for how we mark these various intervals through the day, or even just two or three of them, is not the issue. The point of it, not unlike the point that God was making with the manna, is to keep us revolving back to an awareness of His presence with us and our need for Him on an all-day-long basis.

Everything else throughout the day is pulling us away from Him, making our morning devotional feel like a distant memory, like something that apparently only works if we're in a den recliner, not in the real world. But how much more often might God speak to us if He had our attention not only before breakfast but at 10:00 and 12:00 and 2:00 and 4:00, maybe more. "Then should any occupation keep us away from [prayer]" wrote Jerome, the translator of the Latin Vulgate, "the hour itself will remind us of that duty."[15]

To most everybody else, each day is a haphazard smashup of events and interactions, or else it's a boring slog that has to be gotten through until they can get home in front of the television at night. But to you—to someone who senses the still, small summons of God at a noted handful of precious, planned, important hours of the morning, noon, and night, your day now throbs with the rhythm of God's purpose and His presence.

The Lord has something special out there to say to you. And who knows what hour of the day might be your best time for hearing Him?

But there's something else we can also learn from the important rhythm of dailiness. We can learn to wait. We can learn to be content. If we choose to stay inside the protective boundaries of today, we keep ourselves from being overwhelmed by things too big for us, for things impossible for us to control. A daily perspective quiets the long-term worries and insecurities that generate static around our ability to hear the voice of God. The more deliberately we focus our attention on today and today only—and on God's presence with us at regular moments throughout the day—we can more easily trust Him to do what we *can't* see because we're more aware of how actively He's moving in what we *can* see.

Students of Scripture know the various biographies that form much of the skeleton of the biblical narrative:

- Noah endured cruel mocking and humiliation for 120 years while he constructed the ark.
- Abraham waited twenty-five years before God brought His covenantal promise of a son to life.
- Joseph faced isolation and incarceration for thirteen years in Egypt en route to a prominent position in Pharaoh's court.
- Moses wandered in the wilderness for four decades before ever seeing the promised land.
- Jesus waited thirty years before He began His public ministry.

But what most don't contemplate in recalling such timelines from the Bible is that each of these periods of years and the promises God fulfilled on the far end of them occurred through a one-at-a-time patchwork of individual days. How did Noah, how did Abraham, how did Joseph, how did Moses survive the many thousands of single days they passed through on these difficult adventures of a lifetime?

The answer we know better is how Jesus did it. Even as His ministry began to expand throughout the ancient borders of Israel, Jesus never appeared hurried, never appeared concerned that things might not come together the way His Father wanted if He didn't accelerate His pace. Every day of Jesus's life moved along at a normal walking gait, about three miles per hour, or what Japanese theologian Kosuke Koyama once identified as being "the speed of God."[16]

Most of us would never have been willing to travel at such a restrained and measured clip. We would always have been trying to think three moves ahead of the game. We wouldn't have felt as if we could afford slowing down long enough to recognize the inherent value of today, even if we believed in its importance. We would already be too busy living mentally inside the future we'd been planning for the months and years to come.

Jesus, however, did the opposite. He sought out places each day—"deserted" places—"very early in the morning, while it was still dark," to get away and be alone with His Father (Mark 1:35). And He told His disciples to do the same: "When you pray, go into your private room, shut your door, and pray to your Father who is in secret. And your Father who sees in secret will reward you" (Matt. 6:6). With His presence. With the excited expectation of simply being with Him. Being quiet. Being still. Waiting for Him.

Within . . . each . . . day.

The speed of God is the speed our souls were made to travel. We are made for marching to a daily rhythm, for waiting on tomorrow by squeezing all the juice out of everything God wants to say to us and develop in us today. We cannot be ready for the next day until we've lived this one.

This kind of pacing is what kept the first disciples ready to "receive power when the Holy Spirit has come on you" (Acts 1:8)—those ten days of staying in the upper room, waiting, as Jesus said, "until you are empowered from on high" (Luke 24:49). Time wasn't working against them as they tried to figure out how to pursue their plans for putting the Great Commission into practice. Time was on their side. The dailiness of waiting for Him. Now was not the time for putting a board of directors in place, for setting themselves up as a 501(c)(3) organization. It was time for them to wait on the Lord, to make their patient prayers to Him in the quietness of their room, within the fullness of each day. If not, they may have either given up, run scared, and quit on Christ's mission, or they'd have shot out of there on nothing but the steam of their own power, charging hell with a water pistol.

The everyday waiting is tough, but the everyday waiting is essential. We can miss the Holy Spirit if we insist on hurrying Him faster than each day allows.

What if I offered you $86,400 today, saying you could spend it on whatever you desire, except with one stipulation. You must spend it all today. If you don't, you'll lose it. You don't necessarily have to spend it all, but you can't carry over today's money to tomorrow.

I have a feeling you could do it. You could find a way to match your pent-up wish list with $86,400 worth of purchases, no problem. The Amazon packages would start piling up on your porch within a matter of hours.

Then what if I showed up again tomorrow and made you the same offer? It would sound too good to be true. *$86,400 again? Today?* I'm still sure you could do it, but I think a second shot at it might make you mindful of purchasing more than just the toys, games, and gadgets you'd never been able to afford before. I think you'd start thinking about putting this windfall of cash toward items that are a little more substantial and long-lasting. Bigger picture. Soon you'd be investing in things that carried their value forward. Your choices would become more thoughtful, more in keeping with the goals of yours that go beyond mere greed. You'd get even better at it. More mature. More serious about what matters to you.

But this $86,400 proposal is not exactly a dream sequence. Remove the dollar sign, and it's actually an offer that is sitting on the kitchen table for you every morning when you wake up. God provides you and me a sack of 86,400 seconds for us to put to whatever use we desire. And doesn't 86,400 seconds give us more than enough to be concerned with today?

If we were losing that much money a day, we would be on the phone first thing, trying to find someone who could tell us what in the world became of it and how we can get it back. Well, it's back. Today. And it'll be back again tomorrow, when tomorrow becomes today.

And as soon as your and my walk with God becomes this daily-centric, we will never again let 86,400 opportunities get away from us when we could have been listening for Him. If we'll seek Him at this daily rhythm, we'll make hearing from Him a daily reality.

Chapter 8

WANTING TO BE CAUGHT

Jesus is not a recruiter calling us to "hustle harder" but the Good Shepherd of Psalm 23, calling us to "lie down in green pastures."[17]

John Mark Comer

Besides His written Word, where God speaks most loudly and clearly, He also speaks to us through other avenues. He speaks to us, for example, through people.

When I was a young Christian, feeling called into preaching ministry, I started telling a group of men in a Bible study I was leading that I had a desire to go to seminary. "Seminary? More like 'cemetery,'" they said—where people's fire for the Lord goes to die, where they trade in their spiritual power for intellect.

"What do you mean?" I asked.

"You don't need schooling, man," they said to me. "You have the Spirit inside you. He's all you need."

The following week, I shared this conversation with David Platt, the now well-known author and pastor, but who at the time was just my mentor and friend. What he ever saw in me—a 6'6", 285-pound former addict and alcoholic, driving a black Cadillac CTS with twenty-inch chrome rims and a $9,000 stereo system in the trunk—I'll never know. He walked across the sanctuary one day at Edgewater Baptist Church in New Orleans, where I couldn't have looked any more like a fish out of water, dressed in the black-on-black shiny clothes I was still wearing from my days in the clubs. He looked to be about fifteen years old, even though he was about my age—blonde hair, blue eyes—but he stuck out his hand in my direction and said, "Robby, would you be interested in meeting me once a week to memorize Scripture, study the Bible, and pray?" We got together every week like that for the next two and half years. He was the first person, in fact, who encouraged me to start looking into seminary to begin with. So I said to him, "David, these guys are telling me I'd be making a mistake. What do you think?"

He answered with a story I've never forgotten. It went like this . . .

Two guys venture into the woods to chop down trees for the purpose of clearing a path through the forest. Using the axes they've been given, they immediately start attacking the trees as they come to them, wood chips flying everywhere. But the work is slow, the progress is minimal. Their energy for it is burning out.

Finally, the second man decides to do something different. Rather than continue hacking away with little to show for it, he sits down and sharpens his axe. He hates the time it's costing him. It seems to be taking forever. In fact, the first guy, who's decided to do his best with the dull axe he's been using, is still plowing ahead, leaving his partner in the dust, back with his file and the sparks from his sanding equipment.

But when that blade in his hand has finally become sharp enough to draw blood at the touch, he picks it up, swings it back, and drives it hard and clean into the bark of that next obstacle in his path. *Crash!* The first tree falls. Then another. Then another. Soon he's caught the first man. Soon he's passing him up. Soon, while his partner is bent double, exhausted, ready to quit from the effort each tree is costing him, the man with the sharpened axe is still going strong.

"Seminary education," David said to me, "is sharpening your axe for ministry. Both men may eventually arrive at the same destination, but one of them will get there a lot faster and more efficiently than the other one."

I know that's not a Bible verse, but I know the Holy Spirit spoke to me through it. Through a person. Through my friend David.

He speaks to us also through circumstances. Perhaps the loudest microphone of them all is the circumstance of death. At the death of a friend or loved one, we're brought face-to-face with our own mortality, with the fact that we're not going to live forever. Whether or not we're willing or ready to deal with it, death forces us to apply our spiritual brakes. Everything comes to a stop, at least for the hour of the funeral, where even those who are far from God become open for a few minutes to hearing from Him and choosing whether to follow where He's leading them.

In these ways and in many others, God is always speaking. And He wants us to hear Him. He wants us to experience the abundant life that only comes from being led by His Spirit. But we are not natural-born listeners. We are highly practiced multitaskers. We have a wandering eye for distraction. We have (most of us) an almost physical aversion to sitting still for any amount of time, much less to stopping for even fifteen minutes later in the day to meditate on something we thought He was saying to us through His Word, through a friend, through a circumstance, or through any of the other means He uses to catch our spirit's attention.

So because we each would admit to a long history of making and breaking promises to ourselves about staying close to Him and listening for Him, the truth is, we need some kind of structure to help us. We need a safety net to catch us when we fall into old habits of neglecting God, of zooming past the sound of His voice, of pretending we can get by just fine on our own initiative without His everyday guidance and reminders of His truth. Something to pull us back into rhythm.

That's the role of *repetition.*

One of the things that's helpful to realize about ourselves is that because of our flesh—our "old self that is corrupted by deceitful desires" (Eph. 4:22)—we are incapable of making changes in our lives without God's help. If we try doing it ourselves, whatever changes we think we've achieved will end up being just as unhealthy as whatever we were trying to get away from. "For the flesh desires what is against the Spirit" (Gal. 5:17). That's the only constant we can count on from ourselves, that we will resist the Spirit coming and going.

Doesn't matter what the issue is, that's what happens. We may be able to get our flesh to cooperate with us in not being so materialistic, for instance, but not without turning our new efforts at minimalism into an equally rotten form of comparison with others. Or if we try to do something about our weakness for needing approval from everyone, any progress we accomplish is likely to just end up making us not care what *anybody* thinks. Satan has options for tripping us up in whatever way we decide to take our self-improvement protocols.

So when you and I feel convicted that, yes, we've not been as attentive to the Spirit as we should, and we draw up new spiritual resolutions to help reorient our lifestyle toward being more engaged with God every day, don't think our flesh can't still take it in a crooked direction. The problems that come from being oblivious to God's voice are really no worse than the problems we create by turning our remedies into religious, performance-based activities that don't get us any closer to God than before.

I guess what I'm saying is—when I start talking about building new structures into our lives, about arranging our days and weeks and months to include *repetition*—I think all of us know our tendencies with that kind of stuff. We can get so zoned in on carrying out our new spiritual program that the program becomes more meaningful to us than the purpose we intended it for.

But that doesn't mean the structure and repetition have no value, that we should run from them like a captive broken loose from his chains. And I can tell you why. Because when God had finally gotten His people together at the base of Mount Sinai, after busting them loose from 400 years of soul-killing bondage in Egypt, He set before them a structure of repetition that He knew they needed if they had any hope of keeping their hearts connected to Him.

God's game plan for the Israelites as they prepared to move on from the wilderness and move into the promised land involved basically a rule book and a calendar. In essence, God's gift to the nation was a day planner. *I'm going to plan your days for you so you can focus on hearing from Me.* Not just their days but their weeks, their months, their years, all of it.

Look at the kinds of rhythms He established for them.

- They were to gather manna daily.
- They were to rest weekly.
- They were to worship at the tabernacle periodically.
- They were to follow a festival calendar yearly.

And at every point along the way, as they learned to live by this new rhythm, He provided for them "the pillar of cloud by day and the pillar of fire by night" (Exod. 13:22) as a visual of His everyday guiding presence.

Could they do it wrong? Yes. Could they turn something so divinely bestowed into an empty form of religious ritual? You bet. The pages of biblical history shout a resounding yes. But did those who bucked at the repetition, who rejected God's gifts of structure, ever find the freedom they longed for by idolatrously searching for it everywhere else? No, not by a long shot.

And throughout Old Testament history, when God spoke to wayward Israel in their circumstances, when they woke up and saw how their freewheeling spiritual ways had only led them into a trap, where did they go to seek relief? They returned to the methods for hearing Him and relating with Him that He'd established with them from the outset.

He knows who we are.

He knows what we need.

Just because our flesh has ways of making anything dull and stale, of making it all about us, doesn't mean the old ways are not still our most trusted ways of making our lives all about Him.

Jewish learning is built on repeating a concept, not just hearing it said once. Truths must be given time to marinate in one's mind, like a tea bag steeping in hot water, effusing deeper meaning with each pass.

That's why we find the Sermon on the Mount presented in two ways in the Gospels. Scholars have debated for years whether Jesus delivered His greatest sermon as one cohesive message—the way it's presented to us in Matthew 5–7—or delivered it many times, perhaps in shorter packages, more like the way Luke weaves these same teachings throughout the tapestry of His ministry.

The answer is yes to both. He taught by repeating things He'd already said so that the truth of it could sink even deeper into His followers' thinking, beliefs, and practices.

Something similar happens in Mark 8–10, where Jesus once, twice, three times talked with His disciples about how "it was necessary for the Son of Man to suffer" (8:31), how He would "be betrayed into the hands of men" (9:31), how they would "condemn him to death" and "hand him over to the Gentiles, and they will mock him, spit on him, flog him, and kill him, and he will rise after three days" (10:33–34). He wanted the people closest to Him to realize, when things started happening to Him that seemed chaotically beyond belief, that the events they were witnessing and experiencing were all part of God's choreographed plan for redemption. He couldn't just tell them once and expect them to get it. He knew they needed to hear it again, and again, and again.

That's the ancient method of Hebraic teaching and learning, and it matters to us especially today because of our culture's addiction for hearing new things, new things, all the time, new things. We want *more* information, *more* detail, *more* news on *more* stuff. And not only has this cultural craving become the way we seek to know more about the inane things we're so curious about in the world around us, but it's also worked itself into what we expect whenever we interact with God.

I'm quoting here extensively from a book of mine called *Rediscovering Discipleship* to show why this learned characteristic of ours—this thirst for new things—is detrimental to hearing from God, even when we're actively engaging with Scripture:

> We have bought into the fallacy that we grow by the introduction of new information alone. We focus on new teachings and more information rather than allowing a single teaching to saturate our minds by meditating on it and applying it to our lives. Jewish rabbis taught much differently. They believed that rehearsing older lessons was just as important as, if not more important than, learning new ones.
>
> Jews read through the Torah day after day, year after year, repeating the words of God throughout their lives. They were in their Bibles all the time, but their goals were typically different than ours. In the *Shema* (Deut. 6:4–9), parents are instructed to "repeat them [the Word of God] to your children." The word "repeat" is another word for honing, as in sharpening a knife with repeated strokes of a stone or a leather strop. One rabbi is quoted as saying, "One who repeats his lesson a hundred times is not like him who repeats it a hundred and one."
>
> First-century students in a Jewish school would rely on repetition and recitation for understanding, and it was common for students by the time of their thirteenth birthday to have most of the Torah committed entirely to memory. This capacity for memory was made possible by constant repetition.[18]

The same things. Over and over. Going back to the same books. Meditating on the same verses. Meeting Him at the same times of day. Asking the same questions and making the same requests. That's the way we make forward progress in hearing from God.

I don't know how the methodical sound of that cadence strikes you when you hear it, but I think we should contemplate whether our love for new and more things isn't just our flesh's way of not wanting to listen. What if the *new* things we want to hear from God were more readily found from hearing the same things again and again? What if the *more* we want to experience in our relationship with Him came from reading and studying and praying over truths we're already familiar with? What if it's that tenth or hundredth or ten thousandth turn of the diamond that finally captures the one facet of its brilliance that radiates a whole different depth of light into our hearts?

A popular practice developed by the desert fathers of the fourth and fifth centuries was the "Jesus Prayer." One of the earliest mentions of it comes from an Egyptian contemplative named Evagrius Ponticus, known for referring to prayer as the mind ascending toward God. The Middle Eastern preacher John of Antioch—or as he's commonly called, John Chrysostom ("Golden Mouth")—said something about the Jesus Prayer in a letter written around AD 407.

It was apparently an attempt to answer Paul's admonition to "pray without ceasing" (1 Thess. 5:17 KJV). People obviously couldn't pray nonstop every day, nor was that what Paul was laying down as a rule for any serious-minded believer. But in the words of a plaintive, rhythmic prayer with roots from New Testament Scripture, they found a way to draw their attention back to God from whatever diversion or distraction had caused them to lose sight of Him: "Lord Jesus Christ, Son of God, have mercy on me, a sinner."

You hear in this prayer the cries of the blind beggar Bartimaeus, calling after Jesus for healing (see Mark 10:47). You also hear the humility of the tax collector who, in contrast to the haughty Pharisee in Jesus's parable about two men praying in the temple, "would not even raise his eyes to heaven," so aware of His unworthiness before an awesome and holy God (Luke 18:13). "I tell you," Jesus said, "this one went down to his house justified rather than the other" (v. 14). This kind of prayer was one the Lord approved, the kind of prayer made by a heart like that.

Traditionally, it's recited aloud, even if quietly, but also with the added connection of aligning your breathing with each phrase as you slowly express it:

- [inhale] "Lord Jesus Christ" [exhale]
- [inhale] "Son of God" [exhale]
- [inhale] "have mercy on me" [exhale]
- [inhale] "a sinner" [exhale]

But, Robby! That just sounds to me like you're chanting a mantra.

Okay. Well, again, our flesh can turn anything into a meaningless ritual. We have a religious component stamped onto our DNA, and it is just as fallen as everything else in these hearts of ours that are "more deceitful than anything else, and incurable" (Jer. 17:9). Apart from Christ.

So, fine, I'm not saying you should get in the habit of saying the specific words of this prayer, certainly not babbling meaningless phrases like those people who "imagine they'll be heard for their many words" (Matt. 6:7). I'm just saying it's often in the repeating of biblically based prayers, or in the repeating of memorized Scripture verses—like, say, repeating the Lord's Prayer—that our hearts and minds recalibrate to the rhythm of God. We hear Him in the familiar, in the restated, in words that are old and precious but might just hold the next new thing He wants to say to us. If we'll listen through repetition.

Repetition is like the weaving of a net, building it strong by the wrapping and rewrapping, like a spider securing a symmetrical web for a night of expectant hunting. And if we reinforce that net day after day with spiritual rhythms and repetitions that become part of our worship and listening mechanism, the chances go way up that we'll catch something.

So I'll gladly run the risk of being over-repetitive in trying to keep my heart listening for God, more than I worry about the repetition endangering my freedom to think and act for myself. I've thought and acted for myself for a long time, and I can tell you, it's mostly turned out poorly for me.

Only twice in Scripture are we told of people making a charcoal fire. I feel sure you remember the first one. While Jesus was being held for questioning inside the courtyard of the high priest, the people lingering around the outside "had made a charcoal fire, because it was cold. They were standing there warming themselves, and Peter was standing with them, warming himself" (John 18:18). This high-strung apostle who'd raised his fist and said to Jesus, "Even if everyone falls away because of you, I will never fall away" (Matt. 26:33)—"Even if I have to die with you, . . . I will never deny you" (v. 35)—was adding insult to the injury his Lord was suffering, denying he knew Him.

But the Bible lets us smell that fire a second time.

After Jesus's death and resurrection, Peter had decided to take the guys fishing. Some have suggested the lingering guilt over his denying of Christ had left him feeling as though his ministry was finished, so he went back to what he knew best. He at least had to really be questioning how he could possibly have failed Jesus in such epic fashion. But in the middle of that fishing trip, a voice called from the shore. They didn't recognize Him at first—the voice and form of the now resurrected Jesus. But the moment Peter knew who it was, he leapt from the boat and swam hard for the shoreline. And drawing closer, what would he see? What would he smell? The smoke of a "charcoal fire" (John 21:9).

Jesus was recreating the scent of Peter's betrayal. Perhaps He was bringing him back to the source of the problem, wanting

Peter to revisit the place of his pain—*not to hurt him but to heal him*. Not to rail on him but to restore him.

The repetition drew him in. He would never again catch the whiff of a charcoal fire burning in the distance somewhere without being brought back to this moment, to the forgiving look he saw in Jesus's eyes, and to the words that I'm sure he repeated to himself hundreds of times in the years to come: "Simon, son of John, do you love me? . . . Feed my sheep" (v. 17).

If we were reliable enough on our own to keep our love and our devotion to Him burning bright, we could afford to swim freestyle through life without needing any ropes on the lanes to guide us. But God knows better. Better than we know ourselves. Better than we should trust our own ability to stay close to Him, close enough where we can hear Him. He knows what a little structure of repetition and remembering can do to help keep us within the sound of His voice.

Part 4

HUMILITY

Chapter 9

ARE YOU THE BLOOD CLOT TO REVIVAL?

It is doubtful whether God can bless a man greatly until he has hurt him deeply.[19]

A. W. Tozer

Go back with me again to the unsettling spring of 2020 when I first started seeking out the stillness of the porch every night. As I'm sure you recall, it wasn't only COVID and the lockdown that had us all on edge. The streets of major U.S. cities were becoming tense with racial protests. Snags in the distribution chain were triggering supply shortages for everyday essentials. Political divisions in the country, though always an issue, were being strained now to the max by the accelerated rollout of vaccines, along with heated arguments from both sides on how mandatory or voluntary the prescribed dosages should be.

Then, to get the rest of the picture that was playing out around *me*, lay against this national backdrop the problems we were going through locally at our church, particularly the lack of support for my leadership that was really starting to snowball as the year progressed. And not just mine. Most of the people on staff with me were as new or newer to Long Hollow as I was, having come to Middle Tennessee from other places and regions of the country. It had been five years for me, but I think we were all still wrestling to some degree with learning the culture and the community we'd embraced as our new home. We'd become terribly siloed. A lot of things just were not working well.

And to top it off, there was the ever-present personal turmoil that had been chewing me up inside for months. The self-doubt and desperation. The suffocating smoke of spiritual burnout. I genuinely feared my ministry here was coming to an end, that I'd failed at what I'd set out to do, that I was staring down the barrel of an unknown future in the midst of an already unprecedented present.

But the part of me that didn't feel beaten just felt beaten down. I wanted someone to blame. I remember becoming pretty vocal with the Lord in one of those early times of meeting with Him. You could call what I said a prayer, but it was more along the lines of a pity party. I told God He needed to fix the problems with my church. And with my staff. And, while He was at it, fix the problems with our elders and deacons. And all the problems in our country and in our city and anything else I wasn't thinking of. Why wasn't He fixing these things? At least *some* of these things. A little help would be nice here.

But everything began to change for me that night after I'd gotten my grievances out, after I'd lamented to Him about the many problems I was facing. His silence hung in the air for a while, indicating to me that He wasn't in a big hurry to do much, I guess, about this litany of concerns that I'd become so worked up about. But then after He'd patiently sat through my lengthy tirade, I sensed a clear and straightforward response from Him that told me He was a lot more interested in something else that was going on, something I hadn't even bothered to bring up. *The problem*, He seemed to say, *is not with your church, your staff, the community, or the country. The problem, Robby, is you. You are the blood clot to revival coming to your church.*

The same Spirit who consoles us in our griefs also convicts us of our sins.

In God's economy, death precedes life. A person can be reborn but not without dying first. "Truly I tell you," Jesus said, "unless a grain of wheat falls to the ground and dies, it remains by itself. But if it dies, it produces much fruit" (John 12:24). *As Jesus knew better than anyone, the road to glory must first intersect with the cross of Calvary.*

Revival is a reawakening of something dead. God sends revival as He chooses but only to people whose lives meet a certain condition: *death*—the death that means we have died and are still dying to ourselves every day: "Dead to sin and alive to God in Christ Jesus" (Rom. 6:11).

Death is the door to resurrection. The death He died on the cross, in His once-for-all atonement for our sin, continues being the pattern we must follow as we stumble and struggle through life, especially through the difficulties we continue to create for ourselves despite being freed by Christ's sacrifice from sin's enslaving curse and power over us.

And that's where He knew He needed to take me. From my version of life to His much better vision for all our lives. And to get there, the Robby I'd become had to die. Robby's long list of complaints. Robby's own little kingdom. Robby's runaway pride, pointing fingers at everybody else but myself. Ten months before revival could break out in our church, the Lord decided to start breaking things in me. *Breakdown was my only hope of breakthrough.*

The healing breakdown of humility.

Humility is a choice. That's true. We can choose it or not choose it. But to any believer in Christ who is thinking clearly, what other choice is there to make? It would be like the choice presented to a prisoner if the warden came down to his cell, inserted his key in the lock, swung the door open, and said, "You choose," motioning him out into the open hallway. "You can stay or you can go." Easiest choice a person ever made.

Because while humility is technically a choice, the only other choice is humiliation. The consequence of choosing not to humble ourselves—of continuing in our sin, of putting personal interests first, of thinking we don't deserve suffering or persecution, of living for affirmation and recognition—is to live locked up and separated from the freedom of an up-close experience with God. It is choosing to travel the same awful, inevitable trajectory of every infuriating failure of a life on earth. Some choice, huh?

And yet millions of us make it every day. We choose our sins—the right to be our own boss in dictating how we live. We choose our pride—the arrogance of depending on ourselves, our own smarts, and our limited power instead of God and His endless supply for every situation. We choose whatever we think is our best way, our most desirable way, our least complicated way of getting more out of life than He seems willing or able to give us. But tell me, where does it lead us? Where has it led you? What have you and I ever gained from choosing our own path, from believing the lies we tell ourselves that this way, this time, will finally walk us somewhere else besides just into another trap?

Humbling ourselves under the trusted wisdom of God's Word and the guiding hand of His Spirit may be a "yoke" He fits around our shoulders, but it's an "easy" yoke (Matt. 11:30). It may feel confining, but it's an invitation to freedom. It may seem like it interferes with our right to express ourselves and be recognized for our accomplishments, but it's in fact the liberating confidence of being able to go wherever He leads us and be assured there's a purpose behind every step.

We don't choose humility at our own peril. We choose it because it's a gracious gift from God, a gift we learn to appreciate over time after seeing the hell every other choice unleashes on us. We choose it because it comes packaged with everything we ever wanted and just didn't know it. We choose it because walking in truth is our protection against running into trouble.

But it took the long silence and solitude of the porch before I seemed ready to grasp this. Only as He took His pruning shears to my pride did I finally understand I had nowhere else to go and no other voice I could trust except the voice of the Holy Spirit. I realized I was never going to make it out of these problems of mine alive unless I came to the end of myself. Unless I learned to pride myself not in me but only in Him.

According to Isaiah 57:15, God's presence gravitates toward two kinds of places: (1) the "high and holy place," in realms far above us, far beyond us, unattainable for mere human beings to go; and (2) "with the oppressed and lowly of spirit."

The first, of course, is out of reach, places where God lives and has always lived without ever needing us. But though He has existed from eternity in perfect independence from us, His desire is "to revive the spirit of the lowly and revive the heart of the oppressed" (v. 15b)—to bring us to life in the only way a person can really live. And so He comes near. To this second place. To the lowly place. Where humility makes us able to hear Him.

And, man, in the work of humbling myself, did He ever start telling me stuff.

Honestly, I'd already let Him swing the axe at so much of my junk—the drug addiction, the alcohol abuse, so many other things like that—I felt like I wasn't really living with any open sin at the time when I first went out on the porch. But being broken, being humble, will put you in that place where you can feel Him poking at your "hidden faults" (Ps. 19:12), the things you hadn't perceived as being so terribly problematic until He tells you they are.

Like jealousy. Hearing Him tell me I was jealous was a real shock to me. I looked around at the life He'd given me—a large ministry assignment, a discipleship ministry, a beautiful wife, a great family, a lot of books with my name on the front of them. Why did he think I was jealous of anybody?

But since I asked, He showed me. I was jealous if the pastor down the street baptized more people than I did or if his church was growing faster than ours. I was jealous if a friend's book sold more copies than mine. I was jealous if someone's online post about something got more traction than whatever I'd put out there myself. And in showing me all this, I heard the voice of the Spirit say, *I am never blessing your church until you can pray for My blessing on that church or on that person—the one you're so jealous of—as passionately as you ask for My blessing on you. Because this is not YOUR ministry, Robby; it is Mine. This is not YOUR kingdom, Robby; it is Mine.*

I knew that, of course. Yet somehow, I'd never really seen myself that way. As being jealous. But on the porch, I saw it all, or at least as much as He knew I could handle at the time. (He's shown me a lot more since.) It makes me sick thinking about it now, but He was right. I'd played directly into the hands of rock-star Christianity. Comparing platforms. And never being satisfied unless mine was bigger and better than others.

Ever since graduating from seminary, I'd succumbed to the temptation of promoting myself, building my brand, climbing the rungs of our denominational ladder. All for the cause of Christ, of course! But over time, I'd blurred the lines between promoting Jesus and promoting Robby. I'd slowly and subtly forgotten whose ministry, whose kingdom, was the only one that mattered, that His is the only purpose behind anything any of us ever do. I now believe a big part of the reason my ideas for promoting His kingdom at Long Hollow had not caught on for the longest time was because I was subconsciously promoting my own.

On December 22, 2020—two days after the Sunday morning when God had poured out His Spirit in such a dramatic way on our church—we announced another impromptu baptism service to be held that night in our worship center. The agenda was simple: no music, no preaching, none of the typical preplanned forms we equate with having church. No order of service. We would be praying and listening for the Spirit—nothing more—and we would follow His lead. That's how spiritually alive and exciting those days were feeling to everybody.

Ninety-nine people had come forward on Sunday morning. You remember me telling you that. And on this nondescript Tuesday night, two days later, same thing. Eighty-seven more. I baptized deacons; I baptized small-group leaders; I baptized church volunteers; I baptized staff; I baptized some of my closest friends.

When I got home that night, I was so full of joy I could bust. And what does a twenty-first-century preacher do in trying to process this kind of event that happened under his leadership? I went to my Instagram app, of course. To brag on the Lord, of course! But when I tapped the icon to open it up, it wouldn't accept my login name and password. Apparently, while cruising around on social media earlier in the day, I'd clicked on a private message link that had compromised my account. Instagram had locked me out.

For most of the next year, revival fire spread through our church and our people. It seemed something incredible was happening almost every day. And every night, I would feel the tug toward my laptop or cell phone, wanting to pump out some front-row pictures direct from the pastor about what was taking place up at Robby Gallaty's church. But for the entire year, my access to Instagram never cleared up. It took all that time and a lot of tech work to retrieve my account from whoever had hijacked it.

Coincidence? I doubt it.

I call it what I feel sure it was: God's gift of protection for a preacher He'd been growing in humility over ten months of shepherding and solitude but who still couldn't be trusted to steward a revival while simultaneously posting it to the internet. So God took away one of my favorite outlets. And in taking one away, He laid it on my heart to take all of them away.

Throughout the duration of that white-hot season of revival, I completely detached from all the various social media platforms. No uploads. No browsing. No scrolling through comment threads. No fishing in the pond of affirmation. No chance for my pride to edge in and, who knows, maybe even stall out a work of God before it truly found its footing, before it made its way to other pastors, other leaders, and other believers just like us, who were hard at work seeking to become "lowly in spirit."

God cannot (or, maybe better to say, He *will* not) fill a full vessel. We are either full of self or full of the Spirit. It's either one or the other. "The eyes of the Lord roam throughout the earth to show himself strong for those who are wholeheartedly devoted to him" (2 Chron. 16:9), those who have quit playing games with Him, those who have stopped lying to themselves about the rampant pride that's running the show in their lives. But it's hard staying consistent at not growing casual. That's why we need the continual magnet of humility drawing us back to the places where we last left Him. The places where we last heard Him.

I was talking to my boys recently about how recovery works—recovery from substance abuse, from pornography, from other forms of addiction. If a person relapses in whatever area they're trying to conquer, they must go back to the beginning and start over. There are no shortcuts to restoration.

In the ministry of Celebrate Recovery, which I firmly endorse and have seen God use as an agent of healing in so many people's lives, they hand out different colors of chips to mark major milestones in a person's progress toward and through sobriety. The most important of them is the blue chip, the one you receive at the beginning of the journey. It means you're acknowledging the reality of your situation, you're seeking help in overcoming it, and you're surrendering your dependence on yourself, on all your "stop-doing-that" efforts at getting clean. You can't do this alone. It's too big. It's too tangled up in self-deception. By accepting a blue chip, you are starting something new, something different, something beautiful. Something that finally has a shot at working. Because God is working.

But the blue chip you receive at first may not be—probably won't be—the only blue chip you'll ever get. (I relapsed twice before finding long-term sobriety myself.) You're likely to need more of them because starting over is part of the program, not only for recovering addicts but for every Christian throughout his or her story of life. Starting over (and over and over and over) is simply part of walking with a God who is fully invested in the redemption business, who has constructed His relationship with us around the infinity of His unconditional love. The goal is never perfection; it's progression.

We can never stop starting.

We must remain a perpetual beginner.

Because here's what we all know: *Pride* will never stop starting. *Temptation* will never stop starting. They don't get thrown out in the garbage never to come back bothering us again. They keep finding their way in, waiting for just the right time and place to reengage with our old ways and patterns of thinking. So we, too, must never stop starting. Returning to God. Confessing our need for Him. Being brave enough to "break up the unplowed ground" of guilt and shame (Jer. 4:3), of all the things we haven't done well, trusting God's promise to us in Jesus that He will never stop starting over again with us either.

The biblical word for this kind of reentry after failure is *repentance*. And humility is the road that drives us there. Not the prideful pursuit of fixing ourselves. Not the complex whiteboarding of new plans and strategies for working our way out of the messes we've made. Everything with God is simple. Not easy, but simple. "Humble yourselves, therefore, under the mighty hand of God, so that he may exalt you at the proper time, casting all your cares on him, because he cares about you" (1 Pet. 5:6–7). He made you; He loves you; He can do what you cannot. Repent and return to Him. Humble yourself before Him. Start over again with Him. Because *the end of yourself is the beginning of God*.

The beginning of hearing from Him again.

During our months of revival, I had a chance to talk with Don Wilton, who for twenty-five years was Billy Graham's pastor, including the final years of his life. As Dr. Graham's days were nearing their end, he spoke with Don about what he hoped he would say (or rather *not* say) in his message at the funeral: "Don't mention my name at all. Just tell them about Jesus."

"But Dr. Graham," his wise pastor said, "there's nothing wrong with talking about your life. The Bible, you know, speaks often about God using men of deep faith to accomplish His work."

After a long, thoughtful pause, the great evangelist conceded, "All right, Don, you can mention my name. But don't do it too much. Make much of Jesus instead."

I felt such a pang of spiritual conviction when he shared that story with me. Who wouldn't? To not be moved by hearing the humility of a man like Billy Graham would be a clear indicator of pride gone mad in our own heart. But so would hearing this story and thinking that God could never cultivate in someone like us—especially in someone like me, a recovering self-promoter—a similar spirit of humility. Humility and repentance are made to work hand in hand in us. To make all things possible.

So here's me sharing my warts-and-all summary of where I've come from and what I've done in the past to feed my thirst for other's admiration. It hurts to say it but it's true. I've been guilty of sharing pictures of myself alongside popular preachers, authors, or speakers just to show off the kind of people I'm sometimes hanging with. I've been guilty of constantly posting pics and tweets about a new book release of mine, not just to cooperate with the publisher's marketing plan but because I was so bound up in needing my work to be a success. I've even been guilty of reposting on *my* feed someone quoting a clip of me on *their* feed. "Hey, did you hear what Mike said about what I said?" Hard to justify this as a God-honoring exercise.

But here now is me sharing with you some of the truths and warnings I've learned from the Lord and have tried to incorporate into my repentant heart, which—if you're anything like me—could maybe be helpful for you as well, helpful for both of us to grow from.

- The approval of the crowd is intoxicating but temporary.
- Self-promotion feels good in the moment, but it leaves us empty in the end.

- Criticizing others online might make us feel superior to others, but what we think of as keyboard courage grieves the heart of God.

So may we never let our charisma outperform our character. May we never allow our giftedness to outgrow our godliness. And may we never confuse whatever fanfare we receive as being confirmation of our faithfulness. As my mentor R. T. Kendall told me on our first FaceTime call, "The greatest freedom in life is having nothing to prove and no one to impress, being completely consumed with being pleasing to God, to our audience of One."[20] Because the question isn't whether we're trending online but whether we're living with integrity offline. The question isn't whether we're building our own brand but whether we're united with others in building Christ's kingdom.

The ministry can be a seductive mistress, and none of us is strong enough on our own to resist its appeal to our vanity. It's way too easy to fall in love with serving Jesus while we're gradually falling out of love with the Jesus we claim to serve.

Yet it's never too late to humbly repent.

So if you haven't been hearing from God in a while, and yet you're hungry to return and live in unbroken fellowship with Him again, give humility another chance to bring His truth to bear on the current state of your heart. Denying yourself is never easy, but it's the only choice—the repentant choice of humility—that puts you back in the flow of His life-giving presence.

For me, it comes from replacing my own name with the name of Jesus every time I think my reputation is not getting its due. It means laying all my plans and expectations before the cross of Christ, letting Him determine which parts of my agenda need to die and which ones He wants to bring to life. But if He doesn't, I don't try to resuscitate them. That would be me putting myself back in control of things, and that's an option I've learned I can't afford to make anymore.

Are you the blood clot to revival coming to your church, ministry, family, or community? Ask God to reveal it to you the way He did to me.

Give me the truth, Lord, and I will not run and hide from it.

It may kill me to hear it. But it's a death I can live with.

Chapter 10

YOU BECOME WHAT YOU BEHOLD

The church is looking for better methods;
God is looking for better men.[21]

E. M. Bounds

Have you ever noticed how pets and their owners often look alike? Believe it or not, the science will back you up on that. In one study, researchers showed hundreds of adults two different sets of side-by-side photographs.[22] One of the pairings included headshots of real-life dog owners and their pets, while the other contained images of random people along with random dogs. Participants were asked to guess which of the two groupings went together.

And 80 percent of them guessed right. The dogs that were pictured next to their owners really did look a lot like their humans, enough that people who didn't know the two of them personally could still fairly accurately see them as a unit. How come?

The rationale behind this commonly held observation is based on something called the *mere exposure effect*. It suggests we are drawn toward things we're familiar with, things we already know, things that feel natural to us by experience. We prefer things we've already been exposed to, things we've been around through repeated interaction.

So, for instance, couples who've been married a long time will often start to resemble their mate—have you ever noticed that?—at least in some of their mannerisms and the things they say or think about. Even a person's choice of car might bear certain similarities to that individual's physical characteristics. And when someone chooses a pet, as the experiment I just described indicates, there's a better than half possibility they'll pick one that somehow reflects what that person sees when they look at themselves in the mirror. Because that's what feels best and right and most familiar to them.

But this "exposure effect" is more than just a psychological principle. It is a spiritual law. And we see it at work in the centuries-old teachings of the Bible.

We become what we behold.

The problem with pride, which we talked about in the previous chapter, is that it makes us our own obsession. We become the chief focus of our lives. What we think. What we pursue. How we spend our time and resources. How we expect to be treated and thought of. And since these priorities and others like them dictate many of the decisions we make and the habits we develop, they become the drivers of our lifestyle. They determine what we routinely obsess over as we journey throughout our everyday life, which over the years defines our character.

Humility does the same, except that it flips the equation on its head. *God* becomes our focus and obsession. What *He* wants us to pursue and follow. Where *He* wants us to give our attention. Who *He* wants us to serve and lay ourselves down for. And since our character is changed and created by what we consume, this motivation that humility inspires in us—letting God drive what we spend our time doing and thinking about—takes our lives in a whole other direction.

The difference between the two is great—between the heart of the proud and the heart of the humble—but it's based on a single, consistent, repeated decision. What we look at is what we look like.

We become what we behold.

So as you and I take the measure of ourselves on whether we're satisfied with the health of our spiritual life, there's not really any complicated mystery to figure out if we want our relationship with God transformed into something that feels purer and more personal, more powerful, real, and alive. It's captured in two words I've used a couple of times in this book already but that I really want to be sure don't get isolated into any one section of the story or into only one aspect of our lives. They are central to how we become incrementally changed each day into the image of Christ and delivered from the many hypocrisies we've learned to tolerate as being normal and unavoidable today, in an era that's as noisy and busy as ours.

We need *unhurried* and *uninterrupted* time with God. Those two words. Time to simply sit in His presence and behold Him. Unhurried. Uninterrupted.

Paul said it this way, in describing both the results we're looking to capture and the requirement that puts us into position to receive them:

> We all, with unveiled faces, are looking as in a mirror at the glory of the Lord and are being transformed into the same image from glory to glory. (2 Cor. 3:18)

The requirement is to *look*. To gaze long and hard upon the Lord and His greatness. And by "looking," I'm not talking about a casual glance or a quick check-in between meetings. Not just a blanket prayer and a verse-of-the-day snapshot from Scripture while keeping one eye open for the dings and flashes coming from our telephone.

That's what believers do so they can feel better about having done their devotions today. But that's not really spending time with the Lord, is it? And it can never make much, if any, difference in the things we find so unsatisfying about ourselves or the experience of our walk with Him. I'm talking about a long, lingering, quiet, and patient focusing on the Spirit of God. Making yourself still in His presence. Meditating on His Word and on the illumination He provides as you listen intently for His voice.

I'm well aware the idea of *meditation* has become hijacked by Eastern religions to mean something different from what the Bible intends. The psalms speak especially often about meditating on God's "actions" (77:12), meditating on His "precepts" (119:15), meditating on His "wonders" (119:27), meditating on His "promise" (119:148), meditating "all day long" (119:97) on "all you have done" (143:5). That's biblical meditation. But perhaps a better word, if *meditation* just seems too far out there for you, is the thought of *contemplation*. Taking time to notice detail. To recognize streams of connected truth. To look for features, to listen for inflections, to become more and more aware of who He is and what He is like, until you start to notice Him and hear from Him regularly throughout the day. Until His nature becomes familiar to you, a part of you, whenever you think of Him.

And from this requirement of "looking" comes the result of "being transformed." But not because you're responsible for making it happen. That's what makes spiritual transformation so distinct from self-help programs and other methods of improving ourselves. We normally think of seeking change by eating better and exercising more, by switching up our sleeping schedule, by implementing multipoint adjustments we believe will finally crack the code on what's been dragging us down for so long.

But, no, the looking is all we do; the transforming is God's job. He takes on all responsibility for changing us, and, as Matthew Henry said in his Bible commentary from the 1700s, "When by his grace he has wrought in us a love to him, he is well pleased with the work of his own hands."[23]

Here's the simple promise of 2 Corinthians 3:18: Every moment we spend beholding God in His glory, we are changed. A little more today than yesterday. And before long, a lot more than we've ever been before. "This is from the Lord who is the Spirit."

But how is this possible?

In order to understand it better, we need to back up in 2 Corinthians 3 and see this verse within the context of what Paul was saying.

In the days of Exodus, while the recently freed children of Israel were camped safely at Sinai, God would call Moses up on the mountain to speak with him and give instructions for him to follow in leading the people on how to live, worship, and obey Him. But something else was taking place in this interchange between man and God. Each time Moses emerged from one of these encounters, "the skin of his face shone as a result of his speaking with the LORD" (Exod. 34:29). And it kind of freaked everybody out. "They were afraid to come near him" (v. 30).

So Moses began taking a veil with him—some kind of face covering—whenever he met with God in private. During the time while he was there in His presence, he would remove the veil and bask in the glow of God's glory. But when He came back out in public, around the people, he would put the veil over his face until his appearance returned to normal.

The stage now is set for understanding what Paul was saying to the Corinthians. "We are not like Moses," he told them, "who used to put a veil over his face" to keep the radiance of God's reflection from dying out (2 Cor. 3:13). That's not what our experience with God is restricted to being anymore as New Testament, new covenant believers.

Being with Him does not need to end now in a temporary, fleeting change. A short-term transformation. Hot today, cold tomorrow. When a person "turns to the Lord" today, "the veil is removed" (v. 16) because of what Christ has done to open the way for *all* of us to stand in His presence and to behold His glory at close range. The change is permanent. As we look at Him and gaze upon Him unhurried and uninterrupted, "with unveiled faces," the transformation just goes on and on. It stretches from "glory to glory" (v. 18). Progressively better and stronger. Ever deeper, ever richer. Each moment we spend focusing on the Lord and the Lord alone, another layer of who we used to be is stripped away, and another layer of His likeness is added on.

This is the secret our enemy does not want you to know. You don't need to try harder to change; you just need to look longer at Jesus. *The battle for your transformation is not won in the gymnasium of willpower but in the sanctuary of His presence.* The key to becoming more like Christ each day is not found in trying to change yourself but in beholding the One who changes you.

For our twentieth wedding anniversary, Kandi and I took a trip to Italy that we'd long dreamed of doing together. And since it coincided with my latest ADHD obsession at the time—the study of fine art—I was even more excited about getting over there to see some of the works of the great Renaissance masters.

None is more famous, I suppose, than Leonardo da Vinci, one of the pillars of Italian painting. He is widely known for his *Last Supper*, painted on the wall of the former Dominican convent of Santa Maria delle Grazie in Milan. But his most memorable work of all, of course, is the *Mona Lisa*.

For many years of its existence, however, the painting was considered ordinary, obscure, and relatively unimportant—one of many that lived within the Louvre in Paris. But in August 1911, a group of three Italians, led by a handyman named Vincenzo Peruggia, walked into the museum on a Monday while it was closed for maintenance and simply took the painting off the wall. He removed it from its frame, hid it under his coat, and kept it tucked away inside his small Paris apartment for two years before trying to sell it to an art dealer in Florence, in hopes of getting it back to Italy where he and his band of coconspirators believed it belonged.

The media sensation that swirled around the arrest of the Italian art thief and the return of this otherwise unheralded piece of painting brought droves of people flocking to see what was so great about it.

Here's what's so great about it.

Historians believe the *Mona Lisa* was commissioned by a wealthy Florentine merchant named Francesco del Giocondo, and the woman with the now legendary face was his wife, Lisa. But da Vinci in his genius was never one to feel overly motivated by meeting deadlines or working quickly on his masterpieces. He toiled on it for years, revisiting the canvas time after time, employing his signature *sfumato* style to create the subtle gradations of color and tone, of shading and lighting, that progressively brought out the enigmatic smile and the wandering eyes that have become the familiar *Lisa* we know throughout the world.

But to his patron, del Giocondo, this had gone on long enough. He demanded the painting's completion. The bickering kept up for months, for years, with da Vinci unable to take his eyes or his hands away from it. Always looking, always thinking, always seeing another slight touch of shading or lighting or movement—something—that he hadn't noticed before in the image he was trying to capture through oils and brush. With each fresh turning of his focus onto the face of his subject, he saw something else, something new, something that added a further idea to his mind, something he wanted to explore and bring to life at his fingertips. He ultimately gave the down payment back so he could keep the piece for himself.

In total, the work that became the *Mona Lisa* took sixteen years to finish. He'd begun it in 1503; he completed it in 1519.

Great things take time to behold.

Beholding God's glory takes time. There is no other way. What we get if we *don't* spend time beholding Him is not a transformed heart but a hardened heart, a veiled heart, a heart that is not becoming familiar with Him and therefore is not being changed by Him.

Paul talked with the Corinthians about that too. When believers approach the Lord and His Word in only a religious way, not in a spiritual way, "a veil lies over their hearts" (2 Cor. 3:15). Their minds are "hardened" to the truth of who He is and to the transformation only He can bring to life in them (v. 14). As we saw earlier in this chapter, "whenever a person turns to the Lord, the veil is removed" (v. 16). It's removed by the Spirit, removed by the work He supernaturally does when He has our full attention, when our head, our heart, and our hands are all congruent with one another, when we're aligned in complete focus on Him rather than pulled in a million directions by other distractions.

If we focus on the news, our obsession with watching for breaking headlines will change us. If we focus on politics, our obsession with keeping up with Capitol Hill will change us. If we focus on sports, our obsession with football and talk radio will change us. And—let me just say this—perhaps nothing will change a person more for the worse than being drawn toward and focusing on sexually immoral imagery and pornography. Scientists have found that a person's brain chemistry literally changes when he or she consumes sexually explicit content.

But spiritual change works the same way. Except instead of shackling us, it frees us. "The Lord is the Spirit, and where the Spirit of the Lord is, there is freedom" (v. 17).

Freedom to sit with Him.

Freedom to wait on Him and wonder at Him.

Freedom to finally hear Him and be changed by Him.

The reason we aren't being transformed, if we're not, is because we haven't been spending time beholding Him. We haven't been meditating on His goodness, marinating in His sovereign wisdom and love for us. We haven't been simmering in His Word, pondering the glories of His kindness to us in Christ Jesus. We haven't been looking at Him to know Him and to become more familiar with the sound of His voice.

But if we'll show up, He'll show out. He will make the spiritual changes in us by His Spirit that we have never been able to pull off by ourselves.

As I look back over my first few years at Long Hollow, I see a guy who was still an extension of the middle school kid who never felt accepted by people and was always trying to be someone he wasn't. I ought to have won an Oscar for how I could become whatever I needed to be to fit in—most of it just to please others, to be liked, to be popular.

And so, when things started really going south in my ministry, what did I do as someone who struggles badly with wanting people's approval and affirmation? I caved under the pressure of not being the best thing going. I spent a lot of my time focusing on the voice inside my head that was telling me, "No one likes you. No one accepts you. You will never be Brother David. You should've just stayed where you were and not tried doing something too big for you."

But the time on the porch changed me. The time spent dwelling on the glory of the Lord, as opposed to the glory of the pastor, turned down the volume on that annoying drumbeat in my mind and replaced it with the life-changing cadence of biblical truth.

I finally began to apply to myself what I'd known and had taught others all along. My worth was not based on other people's opinions of me. I didn't need to prove anything to people who didn't care about me, didn't need to impress people who didn't even know me. My identity was not defined by comments made in someone's email or by online criticisms posted by someone who'd never met me. My value had been solidified by Christ on the cross. No longer did I need to keep working for God's acceptance; I'd been freed by the Holy Spirit to work *from* His acceptance.

And I learned this not because I'd worked so hard at becoming smarter and wiser than my adolescent self-image sometimes declared me to be. I changed inside because I'd finally spent time—*lots* of time—beholding the glory of the Lord, becoming more familiar with His rhythms, becoming tuned to the frequency of reality, and being transformed by the work of His hand. Not mine.

I don't know how much more clearly I can say it. And I'm not saying it like a know-it-all (because I'm certainly not) but because I just know how much convincing we need. We've been hard-wired to believe growing in our relationship with Christ requires finding the right book and figuring out the right method and taking the right steps. But, no, it takes *one* step. It takes planting our bodies in the presence of God and not getting up until we've gazed and watched and waited on His glory. *Every great movement of God begins by not moving.* Are you willing to say, "God, I'm not going to move until You move in my midst"? Are you willing to say, like Moses, "How will it be known that I and your people have found favor with you unless you go with us?" (Exod. 33:16).

Jeremiah put his finger on it centuries ago when he said of Israel's ancestors, "They stopped asking, 'Where is the LORD?'"—the One who'd "brought us from the land of Egypt" and "led us through the wilderness" (Jer. 2:6). Even the "priests quit asking, 'Where is the LORD?' The experts in the law no longer knew me," God said, "and the rulers rebelled against me" (v. 8).

When we don't know our Creator, we can never understand why we've been created. When we don't know what the one true God is like and what He loves, we will fill up the perceived emptiness with made-up idols, not realizing we've already been given His fullness. The root of all spiritual wandering is forgetting who God is. And consequently, forgetting who *we* are. We focus instead on the expectations of everyone else—the person others want us to be. On imitating others' success—the person the world wants us to be. On our infatuation with money, things, possessions—the person people pay us to be. On our preoccupations of life—the person our available time limits us to being.

If we behold anger, we become angry. If we behold bitterness, we become bitter. If we behold fear, we become fearful. If we behold lust, we become lustful.

But if we're beholding God's love, we become loving. If we're beholding His peace, we become peaceful. If we're beholding His joy and patience and gentleness, we become more joyful and patient and gentler around everyone. And if we behold Him in the beauty of His holiness, we become increasingly "transformed into the same image" by "the Lord who is the Spirit" (2 Cor. 3:18). That's not just *one* way of changing; it is *the* way of changing.

I'm sure you've heard people say, "The way you spell love is T-I-M-E." It's the way you spell change as well. By time spent with God away from everything else.

And I know it because that's how it happened to me. And is *still* happening to me.

When God manifested His presence on us in 2020 and 2021, the way He did at Long Hollow, I was no longer the cocky expert who knew more than all my critics and was blind to how pride had infiltrated my heart and my spirit. I'm not saying I'm cured completely of my tendencies toward approval-seeking and spiritual snobbery. No way. But ask the people who are closest to me. They'll tell you God has changed me into somebody different from the man I used to be. After the season of revival at our church, Long Hollow received a new pastor, I got a new church, and nobody had to leave.

Once upon a time, if you had asked me about what revival was, I would've given you a cataloged four-part answer. And if revival had come to a church I was leading, I would've told you about the program I came up with that made it happen and would hope you mentioned my name when you shared those insights with others.

But I am holding in my hand right now the first entry from the first journal I began keeping during that season, wanting to be sure I got down in writing what the Lord had been teaching me so that I could go back and review it and retain these memories for later. Here's what I wrote:

> My prayer has been that this would not be about me. I don't want it to be about Long Hollow or our staff. I want this to be about Jesus. I'm praying that what happens here will spill over to other churches in America. I'm praying that pastors and believers would believe that God could do the same thing at their churches.

I'm not pretending there's anything spectacular or profound in these words themselves. But what's spectacular to me—to someone who knows me and my history as well as I do, better than anyone else can know it—is that the heart behind these words doesn't sound like me, like the man and the pastor I *used* to be. It sounds like someone who's been set free from the pride that once held him in chains, the pride that almost always seemed to be chattering a lot more loudly in his ear than the worshipful notes of grace and humility.

It sounds like someone who'd spent unhurried, uninterrupted time with God. Because I had. I really had. And because of it, He did something transformative in me, same as He wants to do in all of us.

We don't only *see* Him when we look for Him, just as we don't only *hear* Him when we listen for Him. We become *like* Him. We don't merely behold His glory. We begin to reflect it.

Part 5

FAITH

Chapter 11

A LIFE BEYOND BELIEF

Faith is believing that it is so, when it is not so,
so that it can be so, because God said so.[24]

Manley Beasley

Around the end of summer a few years ago, I arrived at my office one morning and found a letter in my chair. It was addressed from an inmate at a prison in northeast Georgia, just a little south of Chattanooga, where I used to pastor.

"I have a big ask," the writer of the letter said. "I don't know if you know this," he went on, but apparently someone had been sending videos of my sermons down there on a zip drive to a former member of my previous church, and a bunch of the men had been getting together on Sunday nights each week to watch them.

"Again, I know this is asking a lot," he said, "but do you think you could ever come down here in person and preach a revival for us? Pick any time you want. After all, we're not going anywhere!" (I got a kick out of that.)

Truth is, I get requests like this pretty regularly. From all over the country. People know my background—how God saved me out of a high-risk lifestyle as a drug user and dealer—and they'll ask if I can come to the jail and speak. They feel like I can relate to them and them to me, better than a lot of preachers would, which I understand. And I'm always humbled and honored to be asked. But it's just hard to work it into the calendar with everything else going on.

So I was about to add this request to a stack of things for my assistant to decline for me. But as I was refolding the letter to put it back into the envelope, I noticed writing on the other side. A long list of names. Seventy-five personal signatures. The seventy-five men who'd been listening to me preach every Sunday night at Walker State Prison.

That's when the voice of the Holy Spirit lit up inside me, right then. He spoke two things. First, think about how easily one of those signatures on the back of that letter could have been mine. I'd been pulled over by the police more than once during those years when I was mostly up to no good. Only by the grace of God had I not been sentenced to do time myself for drug trafficking. Second, listen to what I was hearing in the sound of this man's words. The same passion and desire, the same faith and teachability that someone once saw in me when I was new to Christ but had no idea how to learn and grow and develop as a new believer on my own.

The same Spirit who sparked an inmate in Georgia to make a "big ask" of a pastor in Nashville sparked faith in my own heart that morning as well. And after months of prayer and years of work and planning, we now have six prisons that are essentially campuses of Long Hollow Church. Additionally, God opened the door to broadcast to 650 prisons through the Pando app, a fantastic tool for getting faith-based content into the hands of people behind bars. We not only encourage them to watch a service together each week, but we're giving them tools to help form life groups and discipleship groups, to journey through the Word together and raise up men who can serve as pastors to the pods of their prison one day.

I'd heard stories like these before. I knew about Jesus saying how one of the marks of His followers is that they visit people in prison and care about their needs. But to really do it, to get our church behind it, even to put a person on staff as a prison church planter—I had no way of knowing how to get something like that off the ground.

But the voice of the Lord said different.

The voice that once called us to faith keeps on calling us to faith again and again.

We have educated ourselves out of dependence on the Holy Spirit. I'm not knocking education. I sought it and loved it and benefit from it every day. But as I once heard someone say, "There's nothing more powerful than telling a story you don't fully understand."

Spiritual life is a daily balancing act. On one side is the knowledge we've gained through studying the Word, a knowledge base we continue to build on and grow into ourselves the more time we spend in Scripture and sound teaching and around the influence of others who know the God of the Bible well. On the other side is encounter, where this knowledge comes alive. Where we put it into practice. Where we listen for the Spirit to speak through this living Word, mix it with our faith and obedience, and apply it in ways that don't feel as safe as sitting and reading by the light of our desk lamp.

That's what we see happening in the eleventh chapter of Hebrews. As you read these summaries of biblical greats from Old Testament days, you realize what made their stories so special—these Bible accounts we all know—was how God led them to believe Him for things they *didn't* know.

They believed God created the world, for instance, "from things that are not visible" (v. 3). Noah acted on a warning of worldwide judgment from God which at the time "was not yet seen" (v. 7). Abraham followed God's command to leave home and head elsewhere "even though he did not know where he was going" (v. 8).

They weren't able to see all these things with their natural eyesight, but "they saw them from a distance, greeted them, and confessed that they were foreigners and temporary residents on the earth" (v. 13). They understood that God's work with them as His followers was not limited to what they could see and learn and deduce from what they knew. He was calling them, like He is calling us, to a life of faith. An *experience* of faith based on our *knowledge* of the faith, without which "it is impossible to please God" (v. 6).

Here, of course, is how the writer of Hebrews sets this whole thing up in the opening verse:

> Faith is the reality of what is hoped for, the proof of what is not seen. (Heb. 11:1)

"Reality" can be translated as *substance—sub*, meaning "beneath"; *stance*, meaning "the foundation we stand on." In no way does authentic faith ever stand on wild guesses, smoke and mirrors, magical thinking, or wishes on the stars. The Bible provides us the scaffolding and the sure footing our faith can rely on. Faith is not a leap into the dark; it is a leap we're expected to take in the light of God's Word.

But it's still a leap. It's *supposed* to be a leap. As James so obediently and controversially leapt out to say under the inspiration of the Spirit, "Faith without works is useless" (James 2:20). The purpose of gaining intellect about the nature and ways of God is not so we can clamp down on what He's allowed us to do but so that we can use this knowledge base as a solid jumping-off point for following Him wherever He leads.

And trust me, He wants to take us way past wherever our intellect is comfortable going.

Our problem mostly is control. We like being in control. That's why we struggle so hard, for instance, with things like silence and stillness. We'd much rather follow a prescribed devotional routine where we're filling the quiet-time space with activities that feel acceptably devotion-like, the ones we've been the most exposed to, the ones we find the most nonthreatening. (Remember the exposure effect?) It's also why we tilt toward having a knowledge-based relationship with God rather than one that deliberately pursues encounters of faith with Him.

And let's just say it—it's why even the idea of a book on "hearing God's voice" is an immediate turnoff to some believers. It's why you may not only be one of the few that picked this book up and decided to try it but one of the few that have made it this far in without saying it's not for you. And I am proud of you for that. Because if what I'm saying is that our experience with God should regularly include listening for the Spirit's voice and following Him where He leads us by faith, I'm saying this because there are lots of us (me included) who really wouldn't mind if it didn't work that way, if we could stay more in charge of this operation ourselves.

But that's not what Noah did, and it's not what Abraham did, and it's not what Moses and David and all the prophets did. It's also not what the early disciples of Jesus did, who ended up being persecuted and imprisoned and martyred for being faithful to do what the Spirit inside them led them to do.

Jesus left us with the Holy Spirit to teach us not only what we need to know but also what to do with it. Because, again, *living* the Bible is even better than *knowing* the Bible.

I know for a fact you've been in situations where all the old templates for encountering God went out the window. You had an impossible problem in front of you, something that was too far beyond you to fix, and you needed to know this Christianity thing was a lot more than just filling out workbook pages and trying not to sin as much. You had a relationship so tangled or a grief so heavy or a panic so terrifying that you were willing to do anything if God would come prove Himself real to you in your life. In real time.

If so, then you know the mind and heart of the dad in Mark 9 who came seeking a miracle from Jesus for his demon-possessed son.

Turns out, Jesus was not around. He was currently on the Mount of Transfiguration with three of His disciples along with Moses and Elijah, where the Father was preparing Him for the ordeal of the cross that was just around the corner.

But some of His *other* disciples were available, believers He had invested with knowledge and power, even specifically the "authority to drive out demons" (Mark 3:15). So this desperate father had every confidence they could help Him in Jesus's place. They knew things. They'd seen things. They'd done things. Surely these companions of the Teacher could do for him and for his family what any other ordinary man on the street could not.

Yet by the time Jesus got there, these guys that He'd left behind with all this spiritual equipment to work with had done nothing. Why? Maybe they just felt like this boy was too far gone. Maybe they'd never seen such a helpless case. Maybe they'd tried performing some of the same strategies that had worked before in situations like these, but for some reason these old methods were not having any effect this time.

All we know for sure is that when Jesus approached them, He gave these disciples one of the strongest rebukes and tongue-lashings we ever hear Him give to His followers anywhere else in the Gospels. You don't really need a Bible commentator to interpret His mood for you. You can hear it and imagine the scene for yourself: "You unbelieving generation, how long will I be with you? How long must I put up with you? Bring him to me" (Mark 9:19). Jesus was not happy. What drove Him to react the way He did?

Powerless disciples. All talk, no action.

Disappointing disciples. All promise, no faith.

Yet sadly, this is us, most of the time. And we don't even know it. What an indictment we can be on the body of Christ. What a poor, pitiful representation of the God we claim to stand for, when people like us who know so much settle for doing so little. Too often the ones who exercise the least faith in Him are those of us who think we're special to Him just because we know more than others do about Him.

The person who showed the most faith in this story—far more than Jesus's own disciples—was the nameless father who brought his son to Jesus to begin with. "If you can do anything," he said to Him, "have compassion on us and help us." And when Jesus assured him, "Everything is possible for the one who believes," the man cried out, "I do believe; help my unbelief!" (vv. 22–24).

There was no phoniness here. No spiritual façade. No lengthy debate on the finer points of whether healing was a realistic expectation or not. Just a confession of inadequacy. Total trust in Jesus. Gut-level faith, honesty, and belief. "Help me!"

And why wasn't it Jesus's disciples who demonstrated that? What was the key indicator that gave them away as being faithless peddlers of biblical realities?

Prayerlessness.

"Why couldn't we drive it out?" they asked Jesus afterward (v. 28). They were now coming around to where He wanted them to be. Their failure in putting their spiritual knowledge to practical use was about to have them ready for learning a valuable lesson. So Jesus honored their desire for being given another chance by telling them the key discipline that they'd forgotten and had been neglecting over time: "This kind can come out by nothing but prayer" (v. 29).

God will know we're truly wanting to hear Him and follow Him by faith when He hears us coming to Him in prayer.

I can't tell you how much I miss Michael Catt. He was senior pastor at Sherwood Baptist Church in Albany, Georgia, for more than thirty years before the deterioration of his health due to cancer and ultimately his death in 2023. The clearest articulation of the size of his faith and vision was captured in the mission statement the Lord gave him for their congregation in the rural Deep South: "to change the world from Albany, Georgia." If you're familiar with some of the major motion pictures that have been birthed from humble beginnings through some of the members of this church over the last ten or twenty years, you know at least a few of the ways God has blessed their boldness in believing Him.

Michael taught me about the power of what he called "Himpossible" prayers. Prayers that have no way of coming to fruition unless God intervenes and acts in our lives. At Long Hollow, we've tried living out this expectation—praying big prayers to a big God—in our own weekly prayer gatherings as a body.

At the beginning of each prayer night, we hand a blank index card to every person as they're walking in. We instruct them to write down on it one impossible request they've been praying for. Then after we've spent the time praying over these individual matters and whatever else the Lord leads us to pray for throughout the evening, we encourage everyone to bring their cards to the front and lay them on the steps of the platform before leaving. Staff members gather up all the cards at the end of the night.

So not only do people receive a blank card each week but also one of the other cards that had been left by a previous participant at a previous prayer meeting. And before we go home, most of those same cards will be back on the stage steps again, only this time they'll include on the back a written name of the person who prayed specifically for their request that night.

I could share with you countless answers to prayer we've seen God deliver to these truly "Himpossible" requests, but one of them always stands out to me. Maria, a Hispanic woman in her fifties, had faithfully attended our prayer nights. Her own desperate request was for her son Robert to be set free from drugs and alcohol and surrender his life to Jesus. Week after week, she prayed for him through tears on the steps of our worship center, while others passed her card around and joined her in believing God was working in Robert's heart through the faith of a praying mother. She and her son hadn't even spoken to each other in months, maybe years, but Maria never gave up hope. And never stopped praying. None of us did.

One night, after I'd asked if anyone had a praise they'd like to share with the group, a young man came down the aisle and stood next to me at the front. Before he could really get the words out, I saw Maria crying uncontrollably in about the third row. She jumped up from her seat, ran toward her son that she hadn't laid eyes on in some time, and threw her arms around his neck. Once the applause of the crowd quieted down enough for him to be heard, he said, "I came here tonight looking for answers. I haven't lived a life that is pleasing to God or my mom. But after being in this place and hearing the prayers of these people, I have decided to give my life to Jesus."

Crazy applause again.

As tears rolled down my face, I said, "Does anyone have Maria's card?" Someone in the back raised her hand and hurried it to the front. When I turned it over, six people's names were listed on the back, each marked by the date when they'd prayed over her seemingly impossible request, when they'd prayed for Robert to hear the voice of God and take his first step of faith. By the following weekend, Robert was in church. He is still serving the Lord today.

I tell you what, that'll increase your faith.

The first mention in the Bible of a word that means "faith" is found in Exodus 17. It's the time when the Israelites were fighting the Amalekites, who would become one of their most challenging and persistent enemies. Joshua was down in the valley, leading the Israelite armies as their field general, while Moses had positioned himself on a hilltop overlooking the battle.

Scripture tells us the encounter went back and forth. "While Moses held up his hand, Israel prevailed, but whenever he put his hand down, Amalek prevailed" (v. 11). So two of the men who regularly assisted him—his brother Aaron and another leader named Hur—came alongside to support Moses whenever his arms became heavy. They stood "one on one side and one on the other so that his hands remained steady until the sun went down" (v. 12).

"Remained steady." This phrase is translated from the Hebrew word *emunah*, meaning "perseverance, steadiness, faithfulness." These men didn't merely believe intellectually that God would bring victory to His people; they responded to Him practically and put their faith into action. They stayed steady through the conflict, trusting the Lord to work through them and their confidence in Him. They stayed in the fight by doing what they believed He had told them to do.

They were like the widow in Jesus's parable about the unjust judge "who didn't fear God or respect people" (Luke 18:2). This woman believed God was able to give her justice against her adversary, even though it required overcoming the unwillingness of a coldhearted court official. And so she kept coming, and kept coming, and wouldn't back down until she'd received what her faith in God had said was hers by right. As Jesus said, by way of application to this story,

> "Will not God grant justice to his elect who cry out to him day and night? Will he delay helping them? I tell you that he will swiftly grant them justice. Nevertheless, when the Son of Man comes, will he find faith on earth?" (vv. 7–8)

Most of us don't pray that much, or at least we don't pray so consistently—for days and months and years if necessary—because we don't really believe prayer works. Let's be honest. We're not convinced God answers. We grow weary and quit because we don't see much need for it, for acting on faith as we're taught in Scripture. We also don't *listen* much in prayer, as if the goal of it is primarily transactional. We don't often realize one of God's chief purposes in prayer is just to draw us close to Him. To keep our hearts attuned to Him. To allow us the experience of living with Him, relating with Him in an ongoing conversation where His Spirit speaks through *logos* truth to give us *rhema* faith assignments.

Faith doesn't say, "I'll get it one day." Faith says, "I already possess it today because God has said it in His Word, and so I'll live like it and act on it." Or, in the words of Manley Beasley that I featured at the top of this chapter, "Faith is believing that it is so, when it is not so, so that it can be so, because God said so."

Manley Beasley's sons, as I've mentioned, have told me how their dad depended on God for everything. I've seen the record of it myself. One of my prize possessions is their father's personal Bible that he used during the late 1970s and 1980s, which his son Jonathan graciously gave me to keep. I treasure being able to trace through those pages to witness how God's Word came alive to him by faith.

He would routinely ask people a question that he asked of himself as well: "What are you trusting God for today?" Today! What are you trusting Him for *today*? Not just with "bless Mom and Dad" and "bless my wife and kids" and other generic, faithless, "bless me" kinds of prayers. What has God specifically been leading you to pray for? He'll tell you if you'll listen. What is He asking you to ask Him that is so far beyond your power to do it or change it or fix it that prayer is truly your only avenue for having any hope of seeing it happen?

Maybe prayer has been hard for you. Maybe you started strong but lost momentum. That's okay—make a commitment right now. While you're studying your Bible today, while you're seeking Him in the stillness today, begin taking the small steps of faith that will lead you to bigger steps of faithfulness tomorrow. As you trust Him first for *one* thing, He will present you with even greater things, even greater opportunities for encountering Him, not only in His Word but in action. In faithful action.

"What are you trusting God for today?"

Don't expect Him to sit silently and not want to talk with you about that.

Chapter 12

THIS MEANS WAR

Is it possible that anyone should set himself to exalt our beloved Lord and not become instantly a target for many arrows?[25]

Amy Carmichael

After the first fifteen weeks of what we were clearly recognizing by then as a supernatural season of revival at our church in 2021, we had baptized more than one thousand people. And we'd met exclusively online for four of those weeks. In the years since, that number has grown to almost four thousand. Some of them were people whom God was calling back to their first love—professing Christians who'd either never been baptized or were realizing they hadn't known what they were doing when they were baptized the first time. Many of them, of course, were brand-new believers, called out of darkness into His marvelous light.

Both the tears and the joys of repentance were flowing through our church in parallel streams. It was like everywhere you looked, you saw people who were broken over their sins like never before and yet were also more alive and refreshed by the grace of God than they ever dreamed they could possibly be.

It was . . . it was awesome.

But here's the part I feel led to tell you. Revival came at a cost. Outwardly, we were witnessing hundreds of people saved and baptized. A church that had been hemorrhaging losses was now growing like crazy. The Spirit was motivating people to pull up stakes and move from all over the place to partner with us in what God was doing here. But behind the scenes, many of our leaders and others in our church were being hammered relentlessly by wave after wave of unimaginable hardships. My wife, Kandi, and I were no exception.

The onslaught became so intense, so incessant, and so seemingly targeted that it could hardly be explained away as just a string of bad luck. Something spiritually significant was going on. In fact, as the pattern became more suspicious, we started keeping a Notes file on my phone of everything that was happening to us. Otherwise, we might not even have believed it ourselves.

One week after the revival began, I went to the doctor about a visible spot that had appeared on my hip. It turned out to be a staph infection. And over the course of the next eight weeks, it only got worse. They ended up needing to cut into me six times to drain the abscess. By the time all was done, it left a dent in my leg the size of a half dollar for me to remember it by.

And our journal only got bigger and gnarlier from there. Cortisone injections in my back left me temporarily paralyzed. A scratched cornea. Carpal tunnel diagnosis in both wrists. Two oral surgeries and two root canals within four months. A torn bicep tendon. Multiple tests to find a reason behind several heart episodes. Ridiculously frequent and expensive home repairs, along with the financial strain left behind in their wake.

Then came the ultimate test. Times two. My closest friend and I, staff member Chris Swain, had decided to go to a local baseball game on a Friday night in July. Both of our families were out of town, and we wanted to take advantage of the opening in our schedules to enjoy some hang time, just us guys. He texted me a little after 5:30 to say he was heading out to walk the dog, and he'd be coming over to meet me right after that.

No more than fifteen minutes later, a neighbor saw him on the ground near his mailbox, not moving. Despite heroic efforts on the scene, and despite a weeklong, around-the-clock vigil at his hospital bed, we watched along with his wife, Melissa, as she made the difficult decision to remove her husband from life support.

Chris was only forty-seven years old.

Kandi and I drove home exhausted that Friday afternoon, more emotionally, spiritually, mentally, and physically spent than we'd ever felt in our lives. After a quiet dinner, we turned off the lights and headed to bed, only to be met with the pulsating flash of ambulance lights in our living room, coming from the direction of the mother-in-law suite behind our house. EMS workers were busily trying to revive Kandi's dad, who had suffered an emergency health situation himself. Within an hour, we were back in the same hospital, same wing, seeing the same doctors, the same nurses, and receiving the same diagnosis. Within a week, I would perform two funerals: one for my best friend and another for my father-in-law.

I'm not seeking your sympathy by sharing these things. And I'm not here to figure out how all these things fit together or why they occurred in our lives and to the people we love. I just know they did. And I just know they hurt. All I'm saying is that when you start seriously waiting on the Lord, seeking to hear from Him, and responding to His Word by the daring obedience of faith, things start happening in the spiritual realm. And not all of it is pretty and suitable for framing. Some of it makes you wonder what God is doing and why He's allowing it. *But what I've learned about revival is that it makes you both a bull's-eye and a blessing.*

I've also learned (and trust me, I don't say this lightly) . . .

The war is worth it.

During my first semester of seminary, I took a class called "Proclaiming the Bible," taught by Dr. Jim Shaddix. The purpose of this course was to teach us how to apply the text of Scripture to a present-day audience.

In order to do this well, it's important to remember the Bible was written *for* us but not *to* us, meaning our best way of interpreting it accurately is by first seeking to understand how it applied to the people it was originally intended to reach. Scholars call this the "hermeneutical arch"—a bridge we pastors and teachers attempt to construct for our listeners, spanning from the ancient world into today.

One of the commonly quoted passages that can benefit greatly from this approach is Romans 8:28: "We know that all things work together for the good of those who love God, who are called according to his purpose." On its face, hearing this verse from a distance of two thousand years, it sounds as though one of the benefits of being a Christian is that we can expect God to spare us from ever being overwhelmed by bad things. But to first-century Roman believers who were facing persecution and ridicule and the real threat of death for declaring their allegiance to Jesus, the idea that God owes His people a steady diet of easy living would make them wonder what kind of rock this Paul guy was living under. Suffering and tribulation were just a fact of life for them—*especially* for them—because of how easily their faith in Christ could be construed as making them an enemy of the state.

So the point Paul was making is not that we get to avoid bad things as we journey through life but that God *works* them into something that's good for us—a word meaning "synergy," the merging of two differing or opposing actions into one. God doesn't sanitize our individual stories into being trouble-free zones; He just rewrites the ending by using the trouble and turmoil we experience to help us be "conformed to the image of his Son" (v. 29).

Now we're starting to understand why the Spirit could lead the writers of Scripture to say things like . . .

> Consider it a great joy, my brothers and sisters, whenever you experience various trials, because you know that the testing of your faith produces endurance. And let

> endurance have its full effect, so that you may be mature and complete, lacking nothing. (James 1:2–4)

Pain is important to how God gets us where He knows we need to be. He uses it not as punishment but as a primary means of conforming us into the image of His Son. Not to destroy us but to develop us. It trains us in . . .

- *Dependence on Him* rather than self-sufficiency
- *Compassion for others* who are suffering
- *Patience and endurance* in difficult circumstances
- *Discernment* between what matters and what doesn't
- *Faith* that sees beyond the present moment

Even the ministry of Jesus required pain and pressure as part of preparing Him to carry out His purpose for being here. "Although he was the Son, he learned obedience from what he suffered" (Heb. 5:8). What makes us think we deserve smooth sailing when not even Jesus Himself was allowed to walk through life unharmed?

The pain is not the problem. In fact, it's often God's preferred method of working His goodness into our lives.

And if we'll use it to tune our ears more intently toward His voice, rather than turning it into reasons for anger and complaint, we're almost sure to hear Him speaking to us with a clarity we never would've heard if we'd always been given our way.

But though God can and does use pain to humble us and get through to us and further equip us for our ministry to Him and to others in the future, the fact remains we are under attack from an enemy whose goals toward us are the exact opposite. And "we are not ignorant of his schemes" (2 Cor. 2:11).

I think you know this, so I won't rehash for you what is clearly presented to us in Scripture. But because this enemy of ours is such an experienced liar, as Jesus described him in John

8:44, we are wise to often remind ourselves that, yes, he is real and, yes, he is at war with us.

The word *devil* literally means "slanderer" or "false accuser." His name, Satan, is another word for "adversary." According to Revelation 12, he was an angel who rebelled against God, was "thrown out" of heaven, and "deceives the whole world" as his mission on earth (v. 9).

And he *knows* you. Knows your history. Knows your weaknesses. Knows your tendencies and vulnerabilities. Knows the full catalog of your sins and the strategies that work best against you. Like an opposing football coach, he's compiled extensive game film on you, and he is invested in your defeat when you step out onto the field tomorrow.

But you and I are not defenseless in standing against the spiritual attacks he has lined up to disturb and discourage us. We can "resist him, firm in the faith" (1 Pet. 5:9)—faith that the same God who draws us closer to Him in our pain can also draw a ring of protection around us from our enemy. We don't have to just sit here and take it. We aren't powerless against stubborn sin patterns, even the ones we've been failing to overcome for years. We can ask God to push back against the weapons being forged against us. We are children of our heavenly Father. We are coheirs with Jesus of eternal blessings. We have the Holy Spirit at work inside us, and nothing can happen to us behind His back.

We can "stand" in the day of battle (Eph. 6:13).

But this is an important distinction as you think about spiritual warfare, different from what you've perhaps been taught. The Bible never instructs us to attack or advance against Satan but simply to armor up against him. To surround ourselves in strength. To take a defensive stance. And that's why this subject is worth including in a book on hearing God's voice, because it brings all the things we've discussed into the experience.

It's not about going on the offensive against him but standing strong in the *stillness*. Not about raising a battle cry but heightening our sense of *listening*. Not about hoping we're ready when the enemy turns up the heat but simply making our resistance to him a part of our regular, everyday *rhythm*. Not about placing confidence in our spiritual learning or abilities but relying on the Spirit alone. Always practicing *humility*.

As James, the half brother of Jesus, said, "Submit to God. Resist the devil" (James 4:7).

That's how we take the fight to him.

By taking our stand.

The armor of God is not just a set of spiritual equipment. It's a mindset, a belief system, a way of helping us stay aware of the real fight we're in—a struggle "not against flesh and blood, but against the rulers, against the authorities, against the cosmic powers of this darkness, against evil, spiritual forces in the heavens" (Eph. 6:12).

Because otherwise, we'd forget. Our normal human senses don't pick it up. We think it's all just the way life is. We blame it on ourselves. And on everybody else. But Paul, writing to early believers who were feeling spiritual pressure every day but didn't know what to do about it, gave them a visual for how to defend themselves against an enemy they couldn't see.

Don't worry about fighting him. Just stand strong. In the "full armor of God" (Eph. 6:11).

And do it like me, every morning. All six pieces. One at a time.

1. *The belt of truth.* Before entering battle, a Roman soldier fastened a belt around his tunic, the one-piece covering that otherwise hung loose at the waist. The belt kept him feeling tight and agile, free from the interference the rest of his clothing might create. It also held his weapons in place, making them easy to reach and access. With his belt around him, a warrior felt put together, ready for any challenge he might face today.

Truth does that for us as believers. It keeps us from being thrown off by all the other things swirling around us. In tying all our thoughts, beliefs, and emotions around the central core of truth, we stop being deceived by our own moods or the way things appear, and we start seeing life as God sees it. This shift in perspective is essential for spiritual warfare. Satan, as we know, distorts reality, but truth corrects our vision.

2. *The breastplate of righteousness.* The breastplate was metal body armor that protected a soldier's heart and vital organs from attack. And for believers, this protective shield is said to represent "righteousness." For years, I assumed Paul's meaning here referred exclusively to Christ's righteousness imputed to us at salvation, the blameless purity of God that amazingly becomes our own identity through the work of the gospel. Surely, there is great protection in that! But I now believe the breastplate of Ephesians 6 encompasses even more.

The Bible presents four types of righteousness: *perfect righteousness*, which only God possesses; *relative righteousness*, comparing one person's obedience to another's; *imputed righteousness*, given to us by Christ, as I was just talking about; and *realized righteousness*, actually living a righteous life, making righteous choices. And this, I think—living a lifestyle of integrity congruent with the faith we profess—is what makes the righteousness of Christ feel alive in us. In our bones, not just in our Bibles. "Whoever orders his conduct, I will show him the salvation of God" (Ps. 50:23). The living proof of a righteous life turns belief into experience and turns us off to the lying temptations of the enemy.

3. *The shoes of peace.* Roman military footwear consisted of open-toed leather boots with thick, nail-studded soles, featuring sturdy straps that tied them to the ankles and shins. They weren't running shoes designed for fleeing or pursuing an enemy. Their job was to help the soldier stand his ground when attacked.

In spiritual battle, we stand firm in peace—not the absence of trouble but the confidence that God will keep us whole, that He will preserve us intact, that He will not fail to provide for us and will keep our hearts at rest even under duress. Life conspires against us to keep us restless and unsure, full of questions about the future and never caught up on the things that need doing in the present. And even if not for the changing culture around us, there's the agitation the devil keeps stirring inside us. But "since we have been justified by faith, we have peace with God through our Lord Jesus Christ" (Rom. 5:1). Why be worried about tomorrow when we know the One who holds tomorrow?

4. *The shield of faith.* The shield protected against projectiles being thrown by an enemy combatant. These darts, spears, and javelins didn't usually result in a kill shot, but they could at least injure or slow down a soldier on foot, rendering him less effective.

The "flaming arrows of the evil one" do the same thing (Eph. 6:16). They create distraction. They cause fear. They seek to wear us down, break our stride, hinder our progress, and make us doubt we'll survive. But not if we slip our arm by faith inside the faithfulness of God. Not if we hold firm to His promise that He will protect us, sustain us, shelter us, and walk us through every circumstance, through every challenge. "The one who lives under the protection of the Most High dwells in the shadow of the Almighty," where His "faithfulness" covers us like a "protective shield" (Ps. 91:1, 4).

5. *The helmet of salvation.* The helmet, of course, guarded the soldier's head, allowing him to stay alert and on mission. Nothing mattered more than that. His heart might feel fear, his body might feel pain, but his mind had to remain focused on the task and on the path that led to victory.

We must continually preach the truth of God's Word to ourselves, the truth that says we are "saved by grace through faith" (Eph. 2:8). We don't achieve it; we receive it. God gives it to us through the finished work of Christ on the cross. So despite our sins and imperfections, we are not defeated victims. Despite the enemy's attempts at making a case against us, our salvation is safe, sound, and secure. As Jesus said, "I give them eternal life, and they will never perish. No one will snatch them out of my hand," because "my Father, who has given them to me, is greater than all" (John 10:28–29). To listen to our enemy, we are less than nothing, but in Christ, we are more than conquerors.

6. *The sword of the Spirit.* As I mentioned several chapters ago, the "word of God" that's equated with the "sword of the Spirit" in this verse (Eph. 6:17) comes from the Greek *rhema*, not *logos*. It's a particular word from God for a specific situation. Think of it as a word *from* God, not just the Word *of* God. Remember, thinking back to what we said about interpreting the Bible, the Ephesian church to whom Paul was writing consisted mainly of Gentiles who were not familiar with the Old Testament Scriptures. But we as believers living today, having the written Word of God readily available to us, are doubly blessed. We can stand on the foundation of the Bible that's been given to us while also receiving and acting upon the Bible-based direction of the Holy Spirit. We can count on Him, as we listen for Him, to communicate specific truths to us that are relevant to the present situations in our lives.

All these pieces of spiritual armor join together to protect our hearts from discontentment and discouragement. To guard our homes, families, and churches from discord and disunity. And to keep our faith from being dismantled by the deceptions of the enemy.

We are weak but our armor is strong.

And with its strength around us, we will stand.*

So is it painful? Is it profitable?

Or is it warfare? Is it pure evil?

Should we simply submit to it? Whatever we're facing?

Or should we stand and fight it? Whatever it takes?

The beauty of what Paul described as being our plan of defense against spiritual attack is that it works just as well in keeping us listening for God's voice in our pain.

* See Appendix 2 for specific prayers when putting on your spiritual armor.

- When we fasten the belt of *truth*, we're committing to see things the way God sees them.
- When we put on the breastplate of *righteousness*, we're choosing to obey and follow His commands.
- When we lace up the shoes of *peace*, we're resting in what Christ has accomplished for us.
- When we raise the shield of *faith*, we're trusting in His promises and history of faithfulness.
- When we secure the helmet of *salvation*, we're embracing our redeemed identity in Christ.
- When we take up the sword of the *Spirit*, we're immersing ourselves in the Word of God.

And when we "pray at all times in the Spirit with every prayer and request, and stay alert with all perseverance and intercession for all the saints" (Eph. 6:18), we are practicing the same faith that both believes in God for protection and relies on Him for perseverance.

So the answer to those questions I asked you at the beginning of this final section is that it doesn't really matter. Whether it's pain or whether it's warfare is not our burden to figure out. Because we're trusting Him by faith either way, no matter where the struggle is coming from. We're standing not in our own strength but in the power of the living God. We can be bold in believing Him to protect us from anything that would damage our testimony or bring dishonor to His name, even while we practice the everyday faith and humility that knows "all things work together for the good of those who love God, who are called according to his purpose" (Rom. 8:28).

The pain we face is real, but it is not without purpose.

The warfare we face is real, but we are not without defense.

And even so, whichever of these conditions is bringing the most pressure on us today, a day is coming on the soon horizon when He "will wipe away every tear from [our] eyes. Death will be no more; grief, crying, and pain will be no more, because the previous things have passed away," because the Lord Jesus Himself is "making everything new" (Rev. 21:4–5).

Till then, we suit up for real life each morning. Not just with the words we speak. We visually picture putting on each piece of the armor before we leave the house for the day.

George Duffield knew the importance of this practice when he penned the words of the great hymn, "Stand Up, Stand Up for Jesus." The third verse explains the process:

> Stand up, stand up for Jesus / stand in His strength alone / the arm of flesh will fail you / ye dare not trust your own. / Put on the gospel armor / each piece put on with prayer; / where duty calls or danger, / be never wanting there.[26]

Our defense is to suit up for battle with the armor God provides for protection today. Then we wait to see—and to hear—how He'll get us through till tomorrow.

Part 6

REMEMBRANCE

Chapter 13

BACK TO THE FUTURE

Practicing the discipline of remembering pulls us out of false stories and back into God's story.[27]

Anne Kerhoulas

At the height of its reign as one of the world's first superpowers, the Persian Empire stretched from the Balkans in the West, across Egypt, through its Middle Eastern hub in what is now Iran, all the way into India. Its original ruler—whose name you'll recall from the latter pages of Old Testament history—was Cyrus the Great, who began conquering neighboring people groups and kingdoms in the region until his vast holdings spanned three continents. He eventually gobbled up the aging Babylonian Empire, even as the Jews were being held in exile there.

By 500 BC, Persian rule had begun expanding westward into Greece, who could do little to oppose them. But at some point, several of the Greek cities that had first begun falling to the empire's control rose up in rebellion, seeking a return to democratic self-rule. And though they were hardly strong enough individually to drive out the occupying forces who'd overtaken them, they sought help from their Greek neighbors across the Aegean Sea to come join them in a worthy fight.

But none of them was willing to invest in an effort that seemed doomed from the beginning, not even the bloodthirsty Spartans. Only the leaders of Athens agreed to send ships and men and support for the cause, which became known as the

Ionian Revolt. It was ultimately unsuccessful, but it did create unnecessary complications and delays in the empire's plans for expansion. The Persians seemed to know they hadn't heard the last of the Greeks. And the current ruler of the empire—Darius I—was determined that they feel the full force of his wrath for their defiance.

Military strategies began forming in the heart of the Persian homeland. They vowed to send armies. They vowed to send navies. They would pillage, kill, confiscate, and destroy. And lest Darius ever be distracted by other matters of state, lest time should ever dampen the zeal he felt when he first heard the news of the Greek uprising and of the people who participated in it, he tasked one of his servants with a simple yet significant obligation. Three times a day, *every* day, while the king's dinner was being served, this attendant was to come up behind him and whisper in his ear a single sentence. A repeated reminder. The same words, every time.

"Sire, remember the Athenians."

One of the key themes of Scripture, all the way through the Bible, is how God understands and deals with this tendency in His people toward forgetfulness.

Time and again, in giving instructions to the children of Israel, He told Moses to tell them, "Be careful not to forget the LORD who brought you out of the land of Egypt" (Deut. 6:12). "Remember that you were a slave" (Deut. 5:15). "Remember what the LORD your God did to Pharaoh and all Egypt" (Deut. 7:18), and "remember that the LORD your God led you on the entire journey these forty years in the wilderness" (Deut. 8:2).

Remember, remember, remember.

Sometimes He told them to remember their failings so as not to repeat them. "Remember and do not forget how you provoked the LORD your God in the wilderness" (Deut. 9:7). At other times, He told them to think back to the battles they'd faced, to the enemies they'd dealt with, and how the Lord had gotten them through. "Remember what the Amalekites did to you on the journey after you left Egypt," how they "met you along the way and attacked all your stragglers from behind when you were tired and weary" (Deut. 25:17–18). Sometimes He told them to keep in mind the events they'd seen with their own eyes or had heard about from others, and to let these happenings from the past serve as warnings for the future. "Remember what the Lord your God did to Miriam on the journey after you left Egypt" (Deut. 24:9).

And this drumbeat of remembrance just goes on and on, even into the Psalms, where the Lord instructs His people not to be like those who "did not remember his power shown on the day he redeemed them from the foe" (Ps. 78:42). Even into the New Testament, like when Jesus emphatically said, "Remember Lot's wife" (Luke 17:32).

Mostly, though, God's appeal to us throughout Scripture is to remember *Him*. "Remember your Creator in the days of your youth" (Eccles. 12:1). "Be careful not to forget the covenant of the Lord your God that he made with you" (Deut. 4:23). "Remember what happened long ago, for I am God, and there is no other" (Isa. 46:9). And perhaps most poignant of all, in words of Jesus that echo down to us through the centuries from His first observance of the Lord's Supper, "Do this in remembrance of me" (1 Cor. 11:24).

Part of our job each day, if we are serious about hearing the voice of God, is to *remember* what we've been rescued from, to *remember* the One who's redeemed us, to *remember* the times when He has shown Himself faithful, and to keep these memories as fresh and real today as when we first experienced them.

As Jesus said to His first followers, trying to summarize everything He'd taught them, "I have told you these things so that when their time comes you will remember I told them to you" (John 16:4). And then "the Counselor, the Holy Spirit, whom the Father will send in my name, will teach you all things and remind you of everything I have told you" (John 14:26).

God is invested in our remembering.
Are we equally as invested in not forgetting?

Eastern cultures, like those from the original lands where the events of the Bible took place, have a long history of approaching life differently from most Western perspectives. While we generally spend the bulk of our mental energy looking forward to what lies ahead, the people of the Bible lived with their backs to the future. They focused more on the past and the present—the things that had already happened and the things they could clearly see.

I'm not saying one approach is better than another; I'm saying we need both. If we modern believers did more looking back and celebrating and thinking about what God has already accomplished, we might not struggle so hard with our faith, our hope, and our confidence in Him. We would hear Him when He speaks to us because we'd recognize His voice from the past. We would develop the spiritual muscle memory we need for trusting Him today by recalling the faithfulness He's shown us in previous seasons of our lives.

God surely had this motivation in mind when, after forty long years in the wilderness, Israel finally stood at the threshold of the promised land. They'd already begun claiming key victories over some of the kings and their territories just to the east of it. The only remaining obstacle to following Him further into the heart of Canaan was the barrier of the Jordan River—normally a manageable stream but not right then, not during harvest season, not while the river ran past them at flood stage.

So there was no way over. Seemingly no way to follow where they thought God was leading them. They'd been waiting their whole lives for it. They'd been told it was theirs. But right now they were stuck. They'd missed their window. There was nothing they could do.

Yet at God's command, Joshua instructed the priests to carry the ark of the covenant ahead of the people, down the bank, and to step their feet into the flowing waters of the Jordan. And then, and there, something miraculous happened. "The water flowing downstream stood still, rising up in a mass" (Josh. 3:16), turning the swollen riverbed into a dry valley, right in front of them. The whole nation, seemingly stranded, was now marching into a promise.

They'd never seen anything like it, not since their parents and grandparents had witnessed the same kind of miracle at the Red Sea. This was their generation's unforgettable moment.

Or *was* it?

Because if it was so unforgettable—if they didn't need help remembering—why would God do what He did next?

> After the entire nation had finished crossing the Jordan, the LORD spoke to Joshua: "Choose twelve men from the people, one man for each tribe, and command them: Take twelve stones from this place in the middle of the Jordan where the priests are standing, carry them with you, and set them down at the place where you spend the night." (Josh. 4:1–3)

Stones. Twelve stones.

Not just little rocks or pebbles, as if they could be carried in one hand or tucked inside their clothing. These were the kinds of stones that took bending at the knees to pick up. I'm sure you could hear the men struggle to hoist them from the riverbed and raise them to their shoulders. God had something special in mind, something that required big things, big rocks, big plans for a big purpose. His first task for His people, after experiencing such a miracle, wasn't drawing up military plans or further scouting the territory. *It was memorial building.* Memory making.

It was time to build a rock pile.

Even big moments, if we aren't deliberate about recalling them, if we're not rhythmic in how we remember them, can lose their sheen after a while. Once they've tumbled around inside each day's cement mixer of current events, once they've been buried under enough years of activity and distraction, we can't quite feel how they felt when we were right there in the middle of them. Not unless we take time to go there. To go *back* there. To remind ourselves.

To remember.

And if that's true of the big moments, the big rocks, think how many other things get lost under the pile. Smaller things, yet still significant things. Times when God was working because He's *always* working. But now they're out of mind, out of focus. As if they never happened.

We *need* these things. *All* these things. We need monuments to God's faithfulness, to answered prayers, to the stories of restoration He wrote into our lives, to seasons when it was so obvious how He was caring for us and paying attention to us and to the people we love—times when His power and wisdom were the only explanations for how those situations turned out the way they did. The only thing worse than not noticing them while they're happening is not remembering them.

We hear Him best, or at least the most often, in the remembering.

The rock pile God decreed to be built on the other side of the Jordan served at least three purposes, the Bible says.

1. *Strength for future trials.* The days ahead would test Israel's faith in ways they could not imagine. Heavily fortified cities awaited them. Giant warriors awaited them. The odds of victory in those battles, based on experience and numbers alone, would repeatedly be against them. But when doubt crept in, when fear threatened to overwhelm them, those twelve stones would stand as silent witnesses to the God who parted the Jordan, the God who does the impossible, the God who keeps His promises. He'd never abandoned them in the past; He would not start abandoning them now. The rock pile told that story.

2. *A sign for their children.* "In the future, when your children ask you, 'What do these stones mean to you?' you should tell them, 'The water of the Jordan was cut off in front of the ark of the LORD's covenant'" (Josh. 4:6–7). God knew children would ask questions. And He wanted those questions to open doors for storytelling, opportunities for parents to testify to their kids about God's miraculous interventions. The sight of those stones, just the fact that they were there, sparked conversations that might not ever happen otherwise.

3. *A sermon for the nations.* Yes, the rock pile and the stories they brought up would primarily be effective in the context of family and community, in encouraging and building up children to look to God for themselves. But to a larger extent, the purpose of these twelve immovable stones was "so that all the peoples of the earth may know that the LORD's hand is strong" (Josh. 4:24). The stones preached a wordless message. They declared that Israel's God was real—different from the gods others worshipped—and He was personally involved in His people's lives. It was evangelism through monument. A testimony that demanded explanation.

The rocks cried out.

They were alive with God's voice.

So when we stack them today, they fulfill the same objectives. When the next trial comes, they help anchor our faith in the tangible reminders of God's faithfulness in the past. When our children see and ask, the stones help us tell them of a God who is not only historically powerful but is presently active. And when the evidence becomes visible to our neighbors, our coworkers, and others who live around us, it gives us ripe and timely moments to share with them about the living God we love and serve and who loves them just as much.

We need such monuments in our spiritual journey.

How big is your rock pile? When someone visits your home or stops in at your workplace, when they observe what's behind you on a video call, what might they see that gives testimony to a God who has acted on your behalf and meets real people in real life? I'm not saying your rock pile needs to be a literal stack of stones, though it *could* be. It could be *anything*.

But in all the ways, both visual and archival, that you and I capture and memorialize God's history in our lives, the Spirit will draw people's attention and work through those "stones" to enable us to speak truth to people. And whether we're recounting to others what He's done for us or simply remembering it ourselves, we will hear God's voice in the encouragement. We will know Him even better by remembering Him.

The difference between knowing *about* someone and knowing them personally is profound. You and I may know details about a celebrity or a sports figure, but we don't have a relationship with them. We don't *know* them the way friends know each other. Too often, though, that's as close as believers choose to get in their relationship with God. But information without intimacy leads to spiritual amnesia, a condition where we not only forget what God has done for us, but we fail to recognize how He's operating in our lives right now. We don't keep our rock pile prominent enough in our vision so that we can easily and regularly keep stacking it higher.

And so we miss opportunities to know Him and to hear His voice, though they are right under our nose, waiting to be discovered.

Here are some of the stones I've tried to gather and keep fresh in my memory:

- *Salvation moments*—the day I came to faith, as well as other moments of spiritual breakthrough, times when God came alive to me in unusually powerful and personal ways

- *Provision stories*—examples of financial help that arrived during a tight season, of ministry opportunities that didn't seem possible, of needs He miraculously met for me
- *Healing experiences*—physical recoveries from sickness and injury, emotional restoration from deep bouts of darkness, relational reconciliation that could only be God's work
- *Protection testimonies*—accidents I remarkably avoided, dangers I somehow escaped, times when the Lord's hedge of protection around me was so vividly evident
- *Guidance instances*—the clear direction He brought to confusing dilemmas, the open and closed doors that revealed His will, the wisdom I received when making crucial decisions

And you've got them too, same as me. The question isn't whether God has made His presence known with this kind of specificity in our lives. The only question is whether we've built into our routine the disciplines that help us remember it. Things like . . .

Keeping a spiritual journal. You may or may not be a natural journal-keeper, but there's no denying the power of returning to those places, putting yourself right back in the moment where you did your best to chronicle what was going on in your life. At the time, you were so familiar with what was happening that you didn't even really need to document it. But because you did, all those fears and feelings that could have been forgotten are all there to revisit. They keep the past alive. They keep the spiritual amnesia at bay. Being able to remember God coming into the valley with you, or to remember the mountain peaks where He took you—something you've perhaps stopped believing is even possible for you—breathes fresh air into your faith today.

Creating family remembrance rituals. "These words that I am giving you today are to be in your heart," God said to the people of Israel. "Repeat them to your children. Talk about them when you sit in your house and when you walk along the road, when you lie down and when you get up." He spoke of treating them like a "sign," like a "symbol" that their kids would instantly recognize, of writing them "on the doorposts of your house and on your city gates" (Deut. 6:6–9). Look for ways to keep your family's history with God a frequent story they're learning to know and to tell by heart.

Practicing biographical reflection. Life offers so many diversions, so many distractions, so many reasons for moving on from the past. But more than you need another podcast to listen to, more than you need another rerun of your favorite sitcom, you need time for reflecting on the highs and lows of your day. How was He present with you? How did He provide for you? Who did He put you around? What did He teach you? This isn't about being too introspective or overthinking everything. It's about making a regular, even daily appointment with Him to spend time listening for His Spirit, asking Him to show you what's most important to remember about the little things that are really the big things.

The cure for spiritual amnesia isn't more information; it's intentional intimacy. It's setting aside these quiet moments to talk with Him and listen for Him. To look for His hand in your circumstances. To create rhythms of remembrance that keep you awake to His activity.

The twelve stones that Joshua ordered to be set up remained in place throughout the whole time that Israel was conquering and settling the promised land. "The stones are still there today," says Joshua 4:9. They stood as enduring proof of what God had done. And what God can do. But somewhere along the way, their significance was lost. The stories stopped being told. The monument became just a big pile of rocks.

In one of the most sobering passages of the Bible, describing a time roughly forty years removed from the day when that stack of stones had first been laid, we're told how "another generation rose up who did not know the LORD or the works he had done for Israel" (Judg. 2:10).

It wasn't merely a case of historical ignorance. The Hebrew phrase that's translated as "did not know" carries a weight of defiance and disrespect toward Him, not simply an unfamiliarity with Him. The same phrase appears later in the description of the wicked sons of Eli, men who certainly knew about God from having grown up around Him but who "did not respect" Him (1 Sam. 2:12), who did not consider Him worth following and obeying.

But if God's people had continued passing down the stories of what He had done, future generations would've been prepared and expected to live by faith and to watch for Him to move. The only reason those stones became meaningless was because one generation stopped making sure their children remembered.

This is the tragedy that befalls many of us, many of our families, many of our churches today. We receive and experience God's goodness, His provision, His healing, His intervention, but we fail to create monuments. We aren't intentional about telling the stories. We may point our children to Bible stories, but we're not pointing them to *our* stories and to *their* stories.

We're not stacking enough rocks.

If we want to hear new things from God, and if we want *them* to hear new things from God, we cannot be lazy about telling and remembering the old things of God.

Do not forget to remember.

Chapter 14

THANKS A LOT

To be grateful is to recognize the love of God in everything he has given us—and he has given us everything.[28]

Thomas Merton

For more than twenty-five years I've suffered from debilitating back pain, following a major car accident in 1999. Having surgery to repair it was just the beginning. In the years since, I've been in and out of the chiropractor's office endless times, undergone tons of decompression treatments, massage therapy, you name it, just to keep me going.

But during the COVID season, as I began sitting on the porch with the Lord every night, whatever muscles and ligaments had been working and fighting to hold all of me together finally had enough. My back just completely gave out, which only amplified the already chronic pain that I'd grown accustomed to dealing with for so long.

Two different surgeons that I consulted both suggested I undergo a procedure to fix what was wrong with me. But in a last-ditch attempt to avoid the operating table, I decided to pursue at least one more cycle of physical therapy to see if it might possibly succeed at making the pain more manageable.

No sooner had I sat down for that first consultation with my physical therapist than he asked me, "So, Robby, do you think your back can be healed?"

What a question, I thought. I'm a preacher. I'm a Christian. Sure, I believe God can heal me, if that's the kind of healing he was talking about. But as far as whether a new, fresh regimen of PT could heal me, I said, "I don't know. I *hope* so. I mean, I can't say I'm optimistic. I've been living with this for so many years, but . . ."

"That's not a good answer," he said.

"It's not?"

"No. Because if you don't believe you can experience healing, then trying to help you is not worth my time. Your mindset affects the outcome."

It reminded me of that unexpected question Jesus asked the crippled man at the pool of Bethesda in John 5. The Bible says this person had been disabled for almost forty years. He'd been seeking a cure for a long time. Yet the first question Jesus asked him was—this blows me away every time—"Do you want to get well?" (v. 6). Stop and think about that. How in the world could there possibly be more than one answer to what Jesus was asking? *"Do I want to get well?" What does it look like? Of course I want to get well!*

But I get it. I see why it's a fair question. Because after a while, after so many setbacks, after enduring so much hurt and damage from wherever you've encountered the most pain in your life—whether physical, emotional, relational, spiritual, or whatever—you can start telling yourself to stop hoping for anything else. You can get stuck inside a broken identity.

So I'd ask that same question of you today. Do you want to get well? Do you think you can experience joy? Do you believe you will ever feel truly loved? Do you have hope that you can overcome a habitual sin or the addiction you can never seem to stop?

Or maybe I'd ask you the question that's been running through this book from the moment you and I set out together at page 1. Do you want to hear the voice of God? Do you believe He still speaks? Are you convinced He wants a closer, deeper, more intimate relationship with you? And do you think you can change your daily habits and requirements enough to make time for developing this kind of relationship with Him where He speaks and you can hear Him? How would you answer, if you're being honest?

And what if the answer to all these questions hinges on one thing?

Gratitude.

You and I and every person who's been redeemed through Christ's blood are faced with three pervasive influences every day that each affect us negatively: the world, the flesh, and the devil. Two of them we can't control. The world system, the world culture, the worldly perspective that diminishes God while elevating man—we don't have a choice but to live here surrounded by it. And the devil, though Christ will ultimately defeat him, and though we've been given spiritual armor to defend ourselves against satanic attack, will never call off the dogs until he and his whole evil enterprise are flung forever into the abyss.

Number one and number two. The world and the devil. We *can* overcome them, but we can't control them.

But then there's number three—the flesh—which is no less formidable a problem to us than the others. Our sinful human nature will be resistant to the Spirit's rule in our hearts from now to the very end. But of the three, our flesh is the one we ourselves have the most influence over. We can tell it what to do, and we can tell it what to think. We can preach the gospel to it, and we can decide whether it lives with its knee bowed down to Jesus.

That's why the most important conversation you'll have today is the talking you do with yourself. Your brain is like a supercomputer, and it runs off the operating system you create from the coding of your internal dialogue. Your self-talk, then, is a self-fulfilling prophecy. Whether you believe you can or can't, you may be right either way. Hear what I'm saying?

Your input changes your outlook, and your outlook changes your behavior. And through the life-changing power and enabling of Christ—by being a branch who abides in that Vine—it puts you in control over your flesh.

So, how's this for something your old sinful, tired, complaining, grumpy, grouchy, pouting flesh needs to hear?

> Let the peace of Christ, to which you were also called in one body, rule your hearts. *And be thankful.* Let the word of Christ dwell richly among you, in all wisdom teaching and admonishing one another through psalms, hymns, and spiritual songs, singing to God *with gratitude in your hearts.* And whatever you do, in word or in deed, do everything in the name of the Lord Jesus, *giving thanks to God the Father through him.* (Col. 3:15–17, emphasis added)

Looks like God's plan for gratitude is to weave it all through our lives.

"Give thanks in *everything*," the Bible says, "for this is God's will for you in Christ Jesus" (1 Thess. 5:18, emphasis added).

I came home a few summers ago from a silent retreat—which, if you've never attempted, is one of the most eye-opening encounters with God you'll ever experience. To force silence upon yourself for even a couple of days, for a weekend, will do more to cleanse you and detoxify you and open your ears to hear from Him than just about anything else you can ever do. It sounds impossible, I know—or maybe it sounds pretty heavenly to you right now, depending on how loud it's been in your world and at your house lately. But if ADHD Robby can sit silently for several days, you can do it too, I promise you. Might want to think about it.

Anyway, during that retreat setting two or three years ago, I felt like the Lord was telling me I needed to change the narrative in my head. You've heard me share with you about some of the severe hardships and difficulties that had wound themselves into that season of revival we were experiencing, as well as some of the tendencies toward burnout that someone with my nature is so highly susceptible to caving under. All of it was real and all of it was painful, but I could choose how I responded to it. And I made up my mind to face each one with a grateful spirit.

Instead of dwelling, for example, on losing my best friend prematurely, instead of feeling cheated by not having any more time to enjoy with him or talk with him, I started rerouting those thoughts and emotions into gratitude. I thanked God for the years Chris and I got to spend together as close friends and the lessons I learned just from being around him.

When I would start to feel weary or impatient with Kandi, who was slowly grieving the loss of her daddy, having to walk through every "first" without him while also needing to comfort her mom, I determined to think differently about those long talks she wanted and how I could resent sometimes what they were interrupting me from doing. Even in mid-conversation, I would sit there silently thanking God for the gift of having her as my wife, cherishing the opportunity of being the one person who knows her the best and with whom she can share her most raw and tender emotions.

And the boys too. Instead of getting upset so often at the challenges involved in raising these two men of ours, I've tried keeping in mind the blessing of having them right here in our home and of the privilege God has given me to invest in their future.

I've stopped focusing on the negatives and become grateful for the positives.

Because they're always there if you look for them.

People who know such things tell us 50,000 thoughts sail through our mind on a given day. *Fifty thousand!* That's a lot of opportunity for being negative, critical, reactive, and aimless. But Scripture teaches us we can "take every thought captive to obey Christ" (2 Cor. 10:5), and we should be thinking only those thoughts that meet the following criteria: "whatever is true, whatever is honorable, whatever is just, whatever is pure, whatever is lovely, whatever is commendable"—things that have "moral excellence," things that are "praiseworthy" (Phil. 4:8).

We should "dwell" on these thoughts, the Bible says—a word meaning to consider, to ponder, to meditate, to focus. Dwelling on them gives us the power of perspective, something people have been needing for as long as people have existed. In Genesis 2, God told the first couple they could indulge from any tree in the garden except for one. Except for *This One*. So, what did they naturally dwell on? What were they consumed with consuming? The one thing they couldn't have. The one thing that would prove deadly for them. Their perception of paradise was tainted by their focus on what was forbidden.

And the same thing happens to us when we fix our attention on what we can't have, on what God has chosen to withhold, on what feels to us to be an unfairness in our lives, a loss we're not willing to live with quietly.

Our perception changes our direction. What we focus on, we become. If we don't deliberately occupy our minds with contentment, with faith, with trust—*with gratitude*—He will not have much to say to us that we are prepared to listen to.

So draw a line in the sand today. Start diverting your eyes away from the things you don't have. Look for opportunities instead to thank God for what you do have. *Gratitude is not about denying reality or pretending everything is fine when it's not. Gratitude is about choosing to see God's goodness even in difficult circumstances.* It's about recognizing the rays of light that are still there to be found, even in the darkest nights.

When you make gratitude a daily practice, something powerful happens. Your focus shifts from what's wrong to what's right. Your energy moves from complaining to celebrating. Your mind transforms from anxious to thankful. Your spirit lifts from defeated to victorious. Your heart changes from bitter to better.

And your ears that have been deaf to the deep and glorious things of God gradually open to the truth, to the joys of being one with Him, to the surpassing wonder of discovering treasure in the last, painful place you would ever expect to find it.

With this goal in mind, I began to keep a "Gratitude Journal," built around three specific prompts I've continued to use in many of my times with God. Often as I sit with Him, I'll seek to remember just three things I can be thankful for:

- *something in my past* that has shaped me
- *something in the present* that brings me joy
- *something in the future* that gives me hope

Just three things. Then tomorrow, three more. And the next day, three more. By the end of the week, I've thought of twenty or so. By the end of each month, I'm pushing a hundred. A hundred new reasons for being thankful instead of complaining. A hundred untapped sources of goodness and blessing. A hundred fresh infusions of worship material.

All because of a simple shift in gratitude.*

Here's the truth. You cannot control everything that happens to you, but you can control what happens *in* you. You cannot change your circumstances overnight, but you can change your perspective today. You cannot rewrite your past, but you can reshape your future by the thoughts you choose to think right now.

Freedom in Christ—freedom to live for Him, freedom to hear from Him—is not dependent on the absence of problems. In many ways, it's dependent more than anything on the presence of gratitude.

For more than twenty years, my back injury defined me. It was my excuse for why I couldn't travel as freely as others.

* See Appendix 2 for sample entries from my Gratitude Journal.

It was my rationale for why I couldn't sleep in a standard-issue hotel bed. It was my go-to for tapping out on things I was afraid would put me in an uncomfortable position. I didn't say it out loud usually; I didn't want others to know what was really behind my hesitance. But internally, to myself, I frequently played this self-sabotaging reel inside my head. It controlled me. It limited me. I continually gave it the authority to force a hard no from me before I'd even asked the Lord whether I should say yes. I started to realize that God never wastes a past hurt in my life. And if He works everything together for His glory, both the good and the bad, then suffering doesn't define me. It refines me into the image of His Son.

What crippling narrative have you believed in *your* mind? Which negative audio file is running on auto-repeat in your own head, hindering you from doing things, from believing all things, from hoping all things, from enduring all things?

"I'm a drug addict!"

"I'm a disappointment!"

"I'm from nowhere!"

"I'm a mistake!"

"I'm broken!"

"I'm a failure!"

"I'm divorced!"

"I'm a sinner!"

None of these labels defines you. None of them is the end-all that draws the curtains on what the Lord wants to accomplish through you. If you believe in His Son, you are not damaged goods but a child of God. You are not a screwup but a conqueror through Christ Jesus. Your past does not define you. Your sin does not define you. You are defined by nothing other than what God says about you.

And He says every believer, like you, everyone who's been adopted into His family, is a joint heir with Jesus. You live with a debit card that's authorized to make unlimited withdrawals from heaven's bank account. You've received a new heart. You operate from a renewed mind. You are a new creation in Christ. You've been set free by the Holy Spirit.

"Thank You, Jesus," is the right response to such a windfall of blessing and goodness. It outweighs whatever else is weighing down your life.

And to agree with what He says about you is to recognize how He speaks.

So choose gratitude. Choose freedom. Choose to believe He is working all things, even those things, together for your good, and choose to trust Him when He whispers to you a different truth from the distorted truth you've been telling yourself.

Say it with me: "Thank You, Jesus."

Say it like you mean it: "Thank You, Jesus."

"Thank You, Jesus."

Part 7

SABBATH

Chapter 15

WELL-RESTED

On the Sabbath we embrace our limits. We let go of the illusion that we are indispensable to the running of the world.[29]

Pete Scazzero

Let's take a breath now. I think you've earned one.

We've come a long way in this book together. And I feel like I've asked a lot of you. But only because of how drastically my relationship with the Lord has changed from His asking a lot of me.

He's asked for *stillness* from someone who is wired for movement and achievement. For *listening* from someone who makes his living by talking. He's asked for daily *rhythm* from a guy whose normal attention span keeps him flying all over the place. And for *humility* from someone who hasn't completely conquered his addiction to approval-seeking pride. He's asked for *faith* from a man who far too often has treated prayer like an optional add-on. And for *remembrance* from someone who is geared toward spending his mental capital on goals that project out years down the road.

And for me, that's a lot. That's asking a lot. How about you?

But why *shouldn't* He ask a lot of us? I realize the work of salvation has already been done by the Lord Jesus Christ. I know our righteousness is "filthy rags" (Isa. 64:6 KJV) and that we can do "nothing" without Him (John 15:5). We are "saved by grace through faith," and nothing else, "not from works" (Eph. 2:8–9).

You were probably already thinking about that verse before I even typed it.

Yet I don't see anybody in Scripture, anyone whose life and testimony I desire to emulate, who didn't pour themselves out for the honor of being His follower. "I labor for this," Paul said—the hard work of gospel ministry—"striving with his strength that works powerfully in me" (Col. 1:29). Though he clearly said, "It is God who is working in you both to will and to work according to his good purpose," he still admonished the church to "work out your own salvation with fear and trembling" (Phil. 2:12–13). As Dallas Willard once said, "Grace is not opposed to effort; it is opposed to earning."[30]

This is no easy walk, being a disciple of Jesus. It's the best life of all. You know that. But it will cost you everything. Don't take another step with Him unless you are serious about living what you say you believe, about prioritizing time with Him, about making your relationship with Him the chief of all your desires.

And yet to enable us to thrive in Him, in order for our spiritual ears to be receptive to hearing Him, He invites us to rest.

No, He *commands* us to rest.

And it might just be the most neglected commandment of all.

My first computer was a 386-SX, state-of-the-art version that, best as I recall, contained about forty megabytes of memory. Even funnier, its processing speed was billed as being light-years ahead of the 16-bit model that came before it, and yet you would laugh today to watch how creakily it operated if you somehow found one that still booted up.

If you're a Gen Xer like me, if you remember the personal computing landscape of the 1990s, you'll remember we were just then expanding our desktop experience to include email and the internet, things like bulletin boards and instant messaging. But gaining access through a dial-up modem to these wonders of technology was painful to the ear. The screeches. The pings. "You've got mail." And once engaged, the connection could be broken by almost anything, usually by a family member picking up the landline phone to make a call in another part of the house.

The only remedy in that case was to reset it, to unplug the modem and wait ten seconds before plugging it back in. Which, if you were forced to do it very much, could be pretty frustrating. But to clever author Anne Lamott, it led to a healthy observation about life that's become a standard quote about the value of rest: "Almost everything will work again if you unplug it for a few minutes, including you."[31]

My life, for years, as I hope I've adequately admitted to you, was a case study on the need for slowing down and abiding in God's presence. "Rest is for the weak," I believed. "I'll sleep when I'm dead." These were the kinds of mantras I lived by. Even now, I can be easily tempted into running at a pace that pushes any Sabbath-keeping of mine way out into the margins.

What about you? How often do you press the reset button on your life? Ever?

All of us, not just ministers, have a tendency to inflict violence on our well-being and to justify it under the banner of doing our best at whatever we do. We work overtime to please or impress people. We handle requests and complaints at all hours of the night. We endlessly scroll social media or whatever else draws our attention away to our laptops, phones, and tablets. We are rarely disconnected long enough to sit alone with the Father.

But God knew this would happen.

He's always known this thing about us.

So He modeled for us the pattern of regular, weekly rest during His seven-day work of creation. "He rested on the seventh day from all his work that he had done," and He "blessed the seventh day and declared it holy" (Gen. 2:2–3). Then many years and adventures later, after delivering Israel from Egyptian bondage, He commanded them to follow His example, to "remember the Sabbath day, to keep it holy" (Exod. 20:8).

You'd think His gift of rest would've been a blessed relief to them. After all, their Egyptian taskmasters had driven them mercilessly at backbreaking, brickmaking work, day after weary day. But like us, the people's history of nonstop work had desensitized them to the possibility, even the privilege, of laying down their tools and obligations for a time. Many of them rebelled against the notion that God would meet their needs if they didn't stay on the job and make the most of the daylight.

But if we don't give Him our rest, we will come apart from the stress. And if we think He will continue chasing around behind us, trying to catch up to us so we can stay within earshot of Him, we will miss the holy whispers that we're zooming past in our zeal for accomplishment.

To watch the spectacle of an Olympic track-and-field event is to view world-class athletes at the peak of their performance. All you see are the lightning strides of the sprinters, the precision handoffs of a relay team—the speed, the skill, the excitement of competition.

But what you *don't* see are the months of training that have culminated in their appearance on this global stage. The weight lifting and extended stretching. The endurance and strengthening drills, the dedicated days to specific muscle groups. The refined diet regimen and the pinpoint timing of each phase of preparation. Everything is focused on having their minds and bodies perfectly ready, funneled down to that precise instant when they explode from the starting block. For those few seconds, for those few minutes, they are producing at maximum energy.

Yet although we don't see it, we kind of know all this. We're not surprised by the extreme sacrifices their craft requires of them. The thing that might most surprise us, however, if we could see them on the days immediately *after* the race, is the same dedication they give to their rest. Essential to their training for the *next* race is the rest they give themselves following *this* race. They work *from* rest, not *for* rest.

And the lives of us amateurs are no different. We need rest for our bodies, rest for our minds, rest for our souls.

As Pete Scazzero says, the problem with many of us during too many seasons of our lives is that our role has outpaced our soul.[32] Our time with the Lord (or more correctly, the lack thereof) is not substantial enough to equip us for our responsibilities. What we do *for* Him is not sustained by our time *with* Him. We have no real way for consistently listening for His voice because everything inside us is always moving in the other direction. We have many outlets but few inlets. We're all exit and no entrance.

We're working *for* rest but not *from* rest.

Think of how most of us typically get ready for vacation. In the weeks leading up to it, we work ourselves ragged trying to get ahead, trying to compensate for the time we're going to be away. Then by the time we get to the beach or the mountains or wherever we most like to go, we're exhausted from all the work we did to get there. It takes us two or three days before we start to feel any relief, which by then is only two or three days away from when it's time to pack up and head home and crank it all back up again.

But what if we instead worked *from* rest, not *for* rest?

This is God's plan for us—a weekly rhythm of rest—which to most of us workaholics sounds like the worst of all possible plans, though it's actually the only plan for getting the best out of us. Let's start here, at His gracious command for our weekly rest, and see where it takes us.

First of all, while it's vital for our soul care that we worship and fellowship with one another in our churches on Sunday, and while I tip my hat to Chick-fil-A for being closed on the Lord's Day, the weekly pattern of Sabbath rest is not confined only to Sunday. Ask me how I know: It's the busiest day of the week for me.

Nothing did more to discredit Jesus's reputation with the religious scorekeepers of His day than His apparent neglect of the Sabbath. Yet He never once downplayed its importance; He merely showed them they were looking at it all wrong. Like *every* command of Scripture, Sabbath is not a checkbox to be legalistically followed but an opportunity to follow *Him*, the "Lord of the Sabbath" (Matt. 12:8).

So don't think of the Sabbath as being a specific day on the calendar. Think of it as a twenty-four-hour period—one of seven we're given every week—to step out from under the normal routine of work and devote it to letting God recharge and refresh your life. As Marty Solomon teaches his children, "Sabbath is no work, we play, we rest, and God loves us."[33]

Now you probably, at first, will not be able to do it. I couldn't either. But remember, the goal is not legalism. Start with something attainable. If your first attempt at buffering a block of time into your schedule for focused rest yields only *one* hour, much less twenty-four, at least that's one hour more than you've been accustomed to devoting to it. That's a win in my book. And if you can increase it next week to four—four dedicated hours of being alone with God, free of distractions, away from technology and social media and all the things that saturate the bulk of your hours every week—that's a win as well. The joy is in the journey.

But the power is in the planning.

If you aim at nothing, you'll hit it every time.

Resting doesn't just happen. If we don't *plan* to rest, the only resting we'll do will be goofing off, and that's not what fills us with fresh energy. That's not what connects us to the frequency of the Holy Spirit. Just as the tradition in Jewish families calls for making preparations on Friday to rest on Saturday, we also need to put thought and effort behind our Sabbath planning.

Here's what I've often done. I've made a list with two columns: on the left, things that are life draining; on the right, things that are life-giving. Resting, for me, means making time for things every week that contribute to my strength of soul.

So on the left, I've listed parts of my weekly activities that, while not completely unenjoyable, simply take a lot out of me. Many of them involve the electronic sorts of connections that are often essential to getting my work done: cell phone, email, laptop, social media. Others include vocational duties: sermon preparation, counseling, even writing this book! I mean, I'm having a good time sharing with you here, but I often feel drained when I'm done with it. I'm ready for a break. I'm thankful for all these things, thankful the Lord allows me to populate my week with them, but I only get worse at them if I don't ever rest from them.

Then there's the right column, where I've listed my life-giving things: Spending time with Kandi and the boys. Reading a book. Going on a walk. Listening to music. Taking a nap. (That's something I used to *never* do.) Reading the Bible. Talking with friends. Disc golf. Drawing. Working in my woodshop. Or working out. When my Sabbath rolls around, I try my best to choose from activities that come from the right side of my list.

Think of your heart like it's a bank account that's been depleted by too many withdrawals through the week. In setting aside time to observe the Sabbath—in keeping it holy—you are creating room for God to make deposits of peace, of His presence, of His sustenance into your spiritual account.

And you are inviting Him to speak. By preparing yourself to listen.

Here's an acronym to help guide your weekly Sabbath, constructed from the letters of REST.

- *Retreat.* Get away for time with God in silence and solitude.
- *Enjoy.* Spend the time just enjoying Him. The goal is to take delight in Him.

- *Stop*. The word *Sabbath* means "to stop, to cease." You're calling work to a halt.
- *Talk*. Sit and converse with Him, with no other agenda than just being with Him.

Doing the important work of just resting in Him.

Years ago, as I've told you, the Lord saved me from alcoholism and drug addiction. (If you're interested in reading about my testimony, see my book *Recovered*.) Today, my more pressing need is for Him to continue saving me from something else: workaholism. So I admit I can go a little overboard when I get on the subject of Sabbath because my need for it feels more acute than maybe yours does. Or maybe not. Maybe you and I are in this together. Maybe we're both as overwrought with overwork as the other, for whatever reason we do it.

But because of this, because I've seen the tangible benefits of observing the Sabbath—in my emotions and my attitudes and in all my relationships, including my relationship with the Lord—I feel as though someone with my temperament might need to experience it even more.

So while I've made a real effort to follow God's command and to keep the weekly Sabbath holy, I've developed what I call a rhythm of "Daily Resets" that help people like me (and maybe someone like you) bring some of that rest and refreshment into all the other days of the week.

For me, these resets consist of fifteen to twenty minutes with the Lord at some segment of each day. And like with the weekly REST model I just now spelled out for you, I've done the same thing with the letters of these everyday RESETS.

Again, it's just sort of a guide, not a directive. It's not like you're taking medicine or needing to follow doctor's orders. But the more concretely I can prepare my expectations for it and write it into my daily narrative, the more likely a man with my workaholic tendencies can keep it up.

I don't make it through all six steps every day. Sometimes I only get through one or two. And sometimes, if I can make the space for it, I might go on for an hour. But I think it's best to think of it, again, as just about a quarter of an hour, stolen from someplace that you might otherwise have swiped up into a mindless escape. And I think we've all got those little slivers of time embedded somewhere within our waking hours.

I always begin by sitting in silence, just for a couple of minutes, asking God to quiet my spirit, to ready my heart for hearing from Him.

Then here we go. Follow along with me.

R—*Relationships.* "Teacher," someone asked Jesus once, "which command in the law is the greatest?" You remember His answer: "Love the Lord your God with all your heart, with all your soul, and with all your mind," and "Love your neighbor as yourself. All the Law and the Prophets depend on these two commands" (Matt. 22:36–40), on these two *relationships*—the vertical with God, the horizontal with others.

So the first reset is to check in on these two relationships that represent the top priorities for a Christian every day. Is my conscience clear before God? Any sin I need to confess? Anything He's leading me to do that I haven't done? Is my love for Him wholehearted today? And what about toward others? Have I wronged anyone? Do I need to ask forgiveness for anything I've done? Is my love for others at full strength today? Of these two greatest commandments, am I focused on following them?

E—*Environment.* "The heavens declare the glory of God, and the sky above proclaims his handiwork" (Ps. 19:1 ESV). If possible from where you are, sit for a moment in silent awe of God's creation. With your eyes open, look around and take notice of it. With your eyes closed, sit quietly and just listen to it.

S—*Stress.* "I am at rest in God alone" (Ps. 62:1), but just about everywhere else, I am uneasy. If I stop and think about it for only a few seconds, I can start to feel the stress of the day in my shoulders and neck. Your body is like a major prophet in your life. It sounds an alarm telling you there's a problem that needs to be addressed. So envision a spiritual MRI scanning your body to identify those places where you need to rest and abide in Him. Ask the Holy Spirit to flood your entire frame, head to toe, with His peace.

E—*Emotions.* "How long will I store up anxious concerns within me, agony in my mind every day? How long will my enemy dominate me?" (Ps. 13:2). All these self-defeating narratives that we allow to play freely in our heads can be crippling. We feel them. We suffer from them. So in this quiet moment, with your mind fixed solely on God, ask Him: "What are the negative thoughts inside me that are doing me no good, that You want to remove? Where is all this fear and worry coming from when You've told me I can walk free from it?" Ask Him to do for you what these feelings say He can never do. Trust Him to be greater in you than whatever your emotions may be telling you.

T—*Thankfulness.* "Give thanks to the Lord, for he is good; his faithful love endures forever" (Ps. 106:1). Neuroscience has shown how a simple shift toward gratitude can rewire our brains, giving us a more positive attitude, more empathy for others, even a stronger physical immune system. Making time for even a brief celebration of gratitude to God, naming one or two specific things you're grateful for, will restart your day like few other disciplines can do. You have many reasons to be upset today; you only need one to be grateful. Adopt an attitude of gratitude.

S—*Scripture.* Finish by meditating on a single verse or passage from God's Word. Go over the passage you've read that morning. If anything lingers in your mind, heart, or body that hasn't been lifted up and let go through the practice of these resets, sink them into the ocean of biblical truth. Receive His refreshment by faith. Turn your emotions over to the corrective light of ultimate reality.

And see if you're not more at rest than you felt just fifteen minutes ago.

The ministry Jesus modeled for us is often the opposite of how we do it. The busier His life became, the more intentionally He retreated. He routinely stepped away from the demands of leadership and from the daily burdens of His calling, seeking time to spend with His Father. To rest and reset. To recover and recharge. To receive what He needed as a man to help Him achieve the ministry He'd been given. The Son, hearing from the Spirit.

Who do we think we are, if we think we're an exception to that rule?

Let's take a deep breath again.

Lord knows we need it.

Chapter 16

WHERE DO WE GO FROM HERE?

I could go on. I usually come to the end of my books feeling like I've completed the outline that I set out to follow. A + B + C = D, and off we go, with everything all buttoned up, ready for action, as though I've said everything I came to say on the subject.

But not this time. As I sit here today, in fact, I'm not even on the porch anymore. Instead of battling the frigid mornings with propane heaters and long johns, instead of sweating out the summer nights with multiple fans that only stir the sweltering heat around, I've traded the outdoor extremes for something more sustainable. I've converted a portable Amish-built garage into what I call my "Silence Shed." The scenery has changed, but the encounters with God have not.

Every night, after Kandi and I have spent some time together catching up, making plans, maybe watching a movie or a TV show together, I venture out to the shed to meet with God—still listening for His voice, still waiting for His direction, still basking in His presence. You'd think after six years of seeking Him this way, it would get easier. You'd think the distractions would subside and the inner negative subcommittee would stop meeting, yet they're as present as they've ever been. I'm continuing to learn that the goal of being with Him is not the absence of thoughts but the presence of God.

I'm still growing. I'm still getting to know Him.

It makes me think again of that favorite quote I shared with you a while back: "There's nothing more powerful than telling a story you don't fully understand." I love that. In a world obsessed with having answers to every question and an algorithm for every problem, I've grown comfortable not comprehending everything about God's work and His ways. I feel as though I've finally been able to internalize something you and I both know, that if He were a God we could fully wrap our minds around, He wouldn't be a God worth worshipping anyway.

I think we even still have no idea just how much deeper He is calling us to come. Sometimes we think we've already traveled a long way—and we have!—but if we only knew how much more of Him we could experience, how much clearer His voice could be, what our lives could really be like if He had all of us, and if all we ever wanted was just more of Him . . .

Truly, we are only getting started. This is only the beginning. Being with Him. Learning from Him. Listening to Him.

But, oh, the places we can go.

If there's one thing I want to leave with you here at the end of this part of our journey together, it would be the one thing I think summarizes my own six-year journey of listening for Him. And it's prayer. I've changed my entire perspective on prayer. *Prayer is not getting something from God; it's getting God.* Our utmost desire should be more of God Himself.

If you're anything like me, your prayer résumé points to you at center stage: *my* wants, *my* family, *my* desires, *my* pain, *my* aches, *my* issues. But prayer is more than getting your agenda into heaven for God to rubber-stamp. It's about God bringing His kingdom to earth through you and through me. It's more about intimacy with a Person than answers to our petitions.

When was the last time, instead of telling God what's important to *you*, you asked God what's important to *Him*?

"God, place on my heart what's on Yours."

"God, help me see the world the way You do."

"God, give me a hatred toward sin like You have."

Let me warn you, these are dangerous prayers. God may just answer them.

But maybe the most important, most liberating thing we can all discover about prayer is that it's not about using the right verbiage or reciting the correct phrases. Some prayers, perhaps the best prayers, transcend words completely. They have no language. They are simply the cries of our heart.

Anyone with children knows what I'm talking about. Imagine putting your newborn in the crib for the night, only to hear him or her yell to you from the baby bed, "Dad, can you come turn the light on for me?" "Mom, I'm starving, would you come feed me?"

Obviously, that's not how infants communicate. Their only form of talking is crying. Yet even without the use of words or vocabulary, their cries say something. And parents (mostly moms) know the language of their child's cry. There's a certain cry for food, another for a tummy ache, another when they're sleepy, another when they're mad. But here's the best news I can share with you: *Our loving Father knows the language of the cries of His children.*

He hears us. He knows us. He recognizes our need in every wail, whimper, and sniffle. He sees our heartfelt pain, discerns the meaning in every teardrop. "We do not know what to pray for as we should, but the Spirit himself intercedes for us with inexpressible groanings" (Rom. 8:26). He knows our silent requests before we ever utter a word.

Charles Spurgeon, the Prince of Preachers, said it best: "The best style of prayer is that which cannot be called anything else but a cry."[34]

Yet as surely as God hears our cry, we can never overestimate the value of silence in communicating with Him, in listening for Him. That would be my other leading takeaway from what He's taught me about seeking Him and hearing from Him: the power of silence, of stillness, of solitude.

Somebody in one of my discipleship groups recently asked me a fair question: "If silence was a hallmark of Jesus's prayer life, why didn't He explicitly teach His disciples to practice it?" Here's my answer: Christ's mission on earth wasn't just to correctly interpret or fulfill the law but to correctly live it out before us. *A theology that can't be lived is a useless theology*, the same way that faith is more than intellectual ascent, that we demonstrate it by our works.

With this in mind, Jesus displayed what a life connected to the Father looked like. He regularly departed from the hustle and bustle of the crowds to get alone with God. But what did He do there? And how did He do it? Did He talk more than listen? Did He sit in silence more than He spoke? What did Jesus's prayer life look like?

He gives us a clue in John 5:

> "Truly I tell you, the Son is not able to do anything on his own, but only what he sees the Father doing. For whatever the Father does, the Son likewise does these things. For the Father loves the Son and shows him everything he is doing, and he will show him greater works than these so that you will be amazed." (vv. 19–20)

I feel sure when Jesus got together with the Father each morning, He probably unpacked the happenings from His previous day. But we know for sure that He also *observed the agenda* for the upcoming day—what the Father was doing, what the Father wanted done. By only doing and saying what the Father desired, Jesus received a direct, daily download from heaven into the hard drive of His heart before carrying out the will of God on earth. That's how and why He was able to respond to each day's situations in a way that was contrary to normal human nature.

Let me show you what I mean.

Mark begins his Gospel with a day in the life of Jesus. After selecting four fishermen to follow Him, Jesus led them to a synagogue service in Capernaum where He served as teacher for the day. But it was no average day. The service was interrupted by a demon-possessed man who identified Jesus's identity before the crowd, something the people had not yet recognized: "I know who you are—the Holy One of God!" (Mark 1:24). Jesus drove out the unclean spirit from the man, right there in the presence of everyone, causing all of them to be amazed at the power, the authority, that accompanied His teaching.

Then after the service, Jesus headed to Peter's mother-in-law's house for a Sabbath rest. Unfortunately, though, she was ill with a fever, flat of her back. Yet Jesus went to her, "took her by the hand, and raised her up" (v. 31). She immediately got out of bed and began to serve them. Soon, word got out to the townspeople that a miracle worker had arrived, prompting the crowds to come flocking to the house hoping to be healed themselves. "The whole town was assembled at the door, and he healed many who were sick with various diseases and drove out many demons" (vv. 33–34).

As you can imagine, then, Jesus was exhausted that night from a full day of ministry. He'd preached a service, He'd been interrupted mid-sermon by a demon, He'd battled the supernatural realm by casting out an unclean spirit, He'd removed an illness from a woman, and to cap it all off, He'd healed every sick and demon-possessed person in town. You would expect the next line in Mark 1 to be, "The following day, Jesus slept in, seeking to restore his energy."

But that's not what it says.

"Very early in the morning, while it was still dark, he got up, went out, and made his way to a *deserted place*; and there he was praying" (v. 35, emphasis added). Jesus understood the importance of departing daily to be alone with his Father—getting still and silent, in solitude and in prayer—not only to renew His strength but to receive His marching orders for the upcoming day.

How do I know this?

Because of what happened at daybreak that morning. Simon searched for Jesus to inform Him about the buzz His ministry was causing throughout Capernaum. "Everyone is looking for you," Peter exclaimed (v. 37). It was as though, in modern terms, the worship team had already sung, the people were poised and waiting to listen, the stage was set for revival, and everyone was just waiting for the preacher to come and kick it off. Most pastors today, hearing a report like that, would've rushed back to get in front of that crowd as fast as they could. But not Jesus. "Let's go on to the neighboring villages so that I may preach there too," He said to Peter. "This is why I have come" (v. 38).

I wish I could've seen the look on Peter's face. Dumbfounded, for sure.

But how did Jesus know to do this? What told Him to deviate from what most leaders would've done? One simple explanation: *His Father had revealed it to Him in prayer that morning.* In the silence. How else would He have known to go against the grain of human desire for preaching to a large crowd that might start a new movement overnight? I believe Jesus spent time alone with the Father so that He would be able to do "greater works" in the days ahead.

He may not have *told* His disciples to go and sit quietly with God in prayer, but His life showed the fruit of it. His example throughout the day proved the power of what had happened in the morning. When He got alone with His Father.

And just listened.

Since that first wave of God's movement at Long Hollow, we've witnessed two more waves of His Spirit wash over us. On one Saturday night, as I prayed over and prepared my sermon for the following morning, God spoke again as clear as day to my heart: *"Offer spontaneous baptism tomorrow."*

As you can imagine, just like before, the timing felt less than ideal. Preparing for baptism the night ahead of Sunday morning can be taxing on my team. But they were used to me following the lead of the Holy Spirit by this point. How thankful I am for a team that is nimble and flexible enough to raise the sail and follow the breath of God wherever He blows. Their response to my late-night text was simple: "We'll be ready for whatever God wants to do tomorrow."

And move He did.

From August to the end of that year, we witnessed almost nine hundred people follow through with baptism. People again began driving in from all over the country. One woman shared how the Holy Spirit woke her up in the middle of the night to drive here and be baptized the next day—from Tampa, Florida. Ten and a half hours. One way.

Another walked up to me thirty minutes after we'd finished and asked, "Is it too late to be baptized? I was listening to your service live while I was painting a house in Nashville. The Spirit spoke clearly to my heart and said, 'You need to drive to Long Hollow to be baptized right now.' Here I am." Countless people testified to driving home after the service only to be instructed by God, *"Go back and be baptized right now."*

Why am I telling you this?

I just think it's time that we all stopped doing and started listening. I think it's time we stopped forcing our own plans to work and started falling on our knees. I wonder how different our lives would be if we adopted a posture of prayer. I wonder how much more clearly we'd align our day around the agenda of heaven if we weren't trying to tell God how to do His job better, if we were just eager to do *our* job, listening for what He's wanting to tell us?

What if we truly gave ourselves to prayer?

What if we gave ourselves to silence and solitude?

What if we made it our priority to listen to Him more and rant to Him less?

Maybe we'd get a word from God tailor-made for our lives. Maybe we'd begin to experience heaven on earth. Maybe we'd experience revival.

And maybe it would never stop.

The porch is ready. The Father is waiting. So where do we go from here?

We go to the place where we wait and hear from God.

AFTERWORD

The story you have just finished reading, the story that Robby has written, is true. I know because I lived it. I watched it all unfold. In real time.

What God did in the life of one pastor, He also did in the lives of a band of believers known as Long Hollow. As I read these pages, there were moments when I even found myself thinking, *This doesn't seem real.* And yet, I assure you—it was. I saw it with my own eyes. I experienced it all.

I have been privileged to serve on staff at Long Hollow for more than twenty years, ten of those alongside Robby. He stepped into a difficult assignment, following a long-time, deeply loved pastor who had battled cancer and ultimately went home to be with the Lord.

When Robby arrived, the church was still grieving. And though the road ahead was anything but easy, he was God's chosen man for the moment. The first five years were tough. There were challenges on every side. But Robby persevered because he knew—without question—that God had called him to Long Hollow.

Then something began to change. Around year five, Robby started spending time on the porch. As the Holy Spirit began the work described in this book, the transformation in him overflowed into the life of our church. Through his leadership, we all began to experience the supernatural, life-giving work of the Spirit in ways none of us had known or had truly experienced before.

This work did not come without resistance. Not surprisingly, the enemy attacked relentlessly. Numerous health issues, house issues, vehicle issues—if something could go wrong, it did. After hearing one story after another, we'd often say, "You can't make this stuff up!" I'm sure there were moments Robby wanted to leave. I know there were times I did—I even begged God to release me. But I never felt dismissed from Long Hollow, and I am profoundly grateful I stayed to witness what all God was doing.

As fierce as the opposition was, we found ourselves in the middle of a wave of revival unlike anything I have ever experienced. I had always dreamed something like this could happen, but I had never seen such a widespread move of the Holy Spirit firsthand. This was different. Lives, many of them, were being transformed before my eyes.

Like Robby said, people drove, flew, even moved from other states across the country because they had watched our services online and sensed the Spirit drawing them to Long Hollow. More than once I thought, *This is crazy!* But it wasn't crazy. It was the mighty presence of God in our midst, a genuine movement of the Spirit, spreading through our church like wildfire. People of all ages were being baptized—coming up out of the water with hands raised in victory or tears streaming down their faces. It was unmistakable. This was not manufactured or manipulated. It was real. God was at work!

Looking back, it's remarkable to see how it all began: on a porch, with a preacher who chose obedience—sitting in the silence and the solitude, night after night, just to wait on God and hear from Him. His obedience changed the preacher into a pastor. And that pastor led a people into an encounter with God that ignited a fire we can only describe with three simple words: *God did it.*

Those days were filled with holy anticipation. Every time we gathered, we wondered what God might do next. No one wanted to miss church, because we knew something sacred was happening.

And the Spirit continues to move. He continues to draw people from all over to be part of what He is doing here. He is directing us into new areas of ministry to impact His kingdom. And we long to keep leaning into Him, leaning on Him, and looking to Him for what He has next.

What I've learned—and what I continue to practice in my own life—are these two things: both *consistency* and *persistence* matter. Every time I pause to "be still and know that He is God," I am reminded that transformation still begins the same way it always has—by repenting, by listening, by obeying, and by trusting God to do what only He can do. For His name and for His fame, may Jesus get ALL the glory!

Julie Woodruff
Executive Adults Minister
Long Hollow Church

Appendix I

CREATING YOUR PORCH: SETTING UP A SPACE FOR SILENCE

I started listening for God on a literal front porch in March 2020. Like I said, though, I've traded the porch now for what I call my "Silence Shed"—a portable Amish-built garage I converted into a dedicated space for meeting with God. But before you think you need to go build something, let me be clear: the porch worked just fine. Your space doesn't need to be elaborate. It needs to be consistent.

Here's what I've learned about setting up a space for silence. These are what I've found to be the essentials.

1. A Designated Place

It doesn't matter if it's a front porch, a spare bedroom, a corner of your garage, or a chair in the backyard. What matters is that when you go there, your soul knows what's about to happen. Over time, the place itself becomes an invitation. Just walking toward it begins to quiet you. My porch did that for me. It became a familiar front porch for my soul—not just a location but a posture.

2. No Technology

Leave your phone inside. I mean it. Not on silent. Not face down. Inside. If you carry it with you, you will look at it. You know this about yourself. The devil's most potent weapon of mass destruction is distraction, and that little device in your pocket is his favorite delivery system.

3. A Bible and a Journal

Bring your Bible for when the Spirit leads you to the Word. Bring a journal for when He gives you something worth writing down. I'd sit on the porch with both my heart and my notebook lying wide open.

4. A Consistent Time

I went out almost every night after we got the boys to bed. That was my rhythm. Yours might be early morning before the house wakes up or during a lunch break. The time matters less than the consistency. Build it into your life the way you'd build in meals or sleep—because it's every bit as essential.

5. Comfort (Not Luxury)

You don't need a temperature-controlled prayer room. But you do need to be comfortable enough that physical discomfort doesn't become one more distraction pulling you away from God. A decent chair. A blanket if it's cold. Water if it's hot. Simple.

So start tonight! Don't wait until you have the perfect setup. The porch was never perfect. It was just available. Grab a chair. Step outside. Leave your phone behind. Sit down for fifteen minutes. And wait to hear from God.

Appendix 2

PRACTICAL NOTES ON SELECTED DISCIPLINES

Psalm 46:10

In chapter 3, I shared with you this simple discipline I use for getting my heart quiet before the Lord every day, slowly quoting and dissecting the words of Psalm 46:10—"Be still and know that I am God." Here are a few more practical notes to help you get started.

- I typically spend two to three minutes on this practice at the beginning of my time in silence. Some days it takes longer. Let it.
- Don't rush this part. Spend time in God's presence.
- If your mind wanders mid-phrase, don't beat yourself up. Simply return to the line where you left off. You haven't failed; you've been given another opportunity to return to God.
- I sometimes work through it differently depending on the day. Some days, for instance, I stop and spend extra time on "know"—asking the Lord, *What do You want me to know today?* Other days I park on "God," and just worship Him for who He is.
- This practice is an on-ramp, not a destination. It prepares your heart for whatever comes next—silence, prayer, the *Examen*, Scripture reading. Use it to transition from the noise of the day to the quiet of His presence.

Putting on the Armor

Below are some prayers you can pray or adapt into your own prayers while you strap on your spiritual armor for the day, inspired by Ephesians 6:11–18:

1. The Belt of Truth

Pray: *Lord, I wrap Your belt of truth around my waist. Ground me in Your truth today. Help me see clearly. Protect me from every lie the enemy would try to pass off as reality.*

2. The Breastplate of Righteousness

Pray: *Lord, I attach the breastplate of righteousness to my chest. Guard my heart today. I don't stand in my own goodness but in Yours. Let my choices reflect who You've made me to be.*

3. The Shoes of Peace

Pray: *Lord, I put the shoes of peace on my feet. Let me walk in Your peace today—not the peace the world gives but the peace that passes understanding. Wherever my feet take me, let me carry Your gospel with me.*

4. The Shield of Faith

Pray: *Lord, I pick up the shield of faith in my left hand. I trust You today. When the enemy fires doubt, fear, and discouragement at me, I choose to believe Your Word over his lies.*

5. The Helmet of Salvation

Pray: *Lord, I place the helmet of salvation on my head. Protect my mind today. I am saved by grace through faith. I am not a defeated victim; I am more than a conqueror through Christ.*

6. The Sword of the Spirit

Pray: *Lord, I grab the sword of the Spirit with my right hand. Bring to my mind the exact Scripture I need for whatever I face today. Let Your Word be alive in me—not just ink on a page but a living sword in my hand.*

7. Prayer in the Spirit

Pray: *Lord, keep me in constant conversation with You today. Not just when I'm desperate but when I'm comfortable. Not just when I need something but when I need You—which is always.*

Gratitude Journal

In chapter 14, on gratitude, I suggested that each time you sit with the Lord, you should seek to remember just three things you can be thankful for:

- ***Something in my past*** that has shaped me
- ***Something in the present*** that brings me joy
- ***Something in the future*** that gives me hope

Below are some sample entries of mine, just to show you how your Gratitude Journal might read.

Tuesday

- Past: The mentor who challenged me to read the Bible in college. That conversation changed the trajectory of my life.
- Present: My son laughing at dinner tonight.
- Future: The hope that God isn't done with the story He's writing in our church.

Wednesday

- Past: The years of addiction that drove me to the end of myself—and into the arms of God.
- Present: A text from a friend who said my sermon helped him forgive his father.
- Future: The promise of Revelation 21:4—that He will wipe every tear away.

Appendix 3

THE H.E.A.R. JOURNAL

I developed the H.E.A.R. Journal twenty years ago to help believers engage more personally and effectively with the Word of God. The H.E.A.R. method and the *Lectio Divina* essentially do the same thing. They slow us down long enough to let God's Word get into us, not just go past us.

Here's how it works. Think of it in four steps.

H—Highlight

As you read your passage of Scripture for the day, listen for a word, phrase, or verse that stands out to you. It might convict you. It might encourage you. It might confuse you. Don't over-think it—just notice what catches your attention. Write it down in your journal. This corresponds to the first movement of the *Lectio Divina*—*Lectio* (Reading)—where the goal is simply to listen attentively for what God is saying through His Word.

E—Explain

Now ask yourself: What does this passage mean? What was the author communicating to the original audience? What is the context? You're not looking for what it means to *you* yet—you're looking for what it means, period. Use any study tools you have. Write down in your own words what this text is saying. This mirrors *Meditatio* (Meditation) in the *Lectio Divina*—chewing on what you've read, allowing the Holy Spirit to connect these truths with your thoughts, emotions, and questions.

A—Apply

Here's where it gets personal. Ask the Holy Spirit: How does this truth apply to my life right now? Is there a sin to confess? A promise to claim? A command to obey? A principle to follow? Write it down with specifics—not "I need to be better," but "I need to call my brother and apologize for what I said last Tuesday." This corresponds to *Oratio* (Prayer) in the *Lectio Divina*—moving from the intellectual to the practical, forming your response to what you've been pondering into a confession, a request, a song of praise, or whatever the Spirit draws out of you.

R—Respond

Close with a written prayer responding to what God has shown you. This is your conversation with Him about what you've just read. It doesn't need to be long or eloquent—it needs to be honest. This mirrors *Contemplatio* (Contemplation)—resting in God's presence, digesting what you've learned, and refusing to rush away from being with Him.

Sample Journal Entry

Date: March 14
Scripture: Jeremiah 33:3

Highlight

"Call to me and I will answer you and tell you great and incomprehensible things you do not know."

Explain

God is speaking through the prophet Jeremiah, who was imprisoned at the time. Even in confinement, God invited him to call out—and promised to respond with things beyond Jeremiah's ability to comprehend on his own. The invitation is personal and the promise is specific: He *will* answer.

Apply

I've been trying to figure out our next ministry season on my own. I keep strategizing and planning, but I haven't really stopped to call on the Lord and listen for His answer. This verse tells me that God wants to reveal things I can't come up with in a staff meeting or from mentors. I need to bring this to the porch tonight.

Respond

Lord, forgive me for running ahead of You. I confess that my planning has become a substitute for listening. You have incomprehensible things You want to show me, and I've been too busy to ask. Tonight, I'm calling out to You. Speak, Lord. I'm listening. Amen.

Tips for Consistency

- Keep your journal next to your Bible. If they're together, you're more likely to use both.
- Don't worry about writing a devotional. No one else needs to read this. It's between you and God.
- If you're using the Foundations reading plan (see versions for all ages at lifeway.com), you'll have a passage already selected for you each day. H.E.A.R. gives you a framework for what to do with it.
- Review your journal entries weekly. You'll be amazed at the patterns the Holy Spirit reveals over time.

ACKNOWLEDGMENTS

Even though a book has one name on the cover, it wouldn't be possible without a team of people.

First, I would like to thank Kandi, my wife, for her constant encouragement and patience with me. Leading up to and during the first wave of the revival, she allowed me to retreat every night to the porch for hours to spend time with God. Because of unjustified pressure I put on myself, I felt the weight of what God was doing at Long Hollow. Not wanting to squelch the revival with something I did or didn't do, I departed often to seek the Lord. Thank you for allowing me to press into God during that season. I wouldn't be the man I am today, nor would our church be experiencing what we have, without your support behind the scenes. Only God knows the sacrifices you've made. I love you dearly.

Working with Lawrence Kimbrough on this project has been an absolute joy. Your recommendation to weave the lessons I was learning into the story in real time took the book to a place I never imagined. You helped me recapture the emotions we experienced during the revival. Your humility and servant-hearted willingness to do whatever it required to make this book the best it could be is something I'm deeply grateful for.

I am grateful for the staff of men and women God has assembled at Long Hollow. Jeremy Brown, Vivian Penuel, Julie Woodruff, Abraham Cremeens, Jeff Borton, Mark Hopkins,

Robert Hutchison, Angie Hurst, and Adam Williams strengthened the manuscript by reading through it with me. I could not have finished this book without your encouragement. It truly is a joy to serve alongside you in ministry.

Finally, I'm thankful for the Lord's kindness toward me during the most challenging season of my life. I am a testament to how His "mercies are new every morning." I am eternally grateful for the salvation I received in 2002 and for the regular meetings on the porch in His presence. Once a person touches the "hem of Your garment," they are never the same. Going back to business-as-usual ministry is a thing of the past. I long for more of Your power and presence each day.

NOTES

1. Blaise Pascal, *Pensées*.

2. Nadia Whitehead, "People Would Rather Be Electrically Shocked Than Left Alone with Their Thoughts," *Science*, July 3, 2014, https://www.science.org/content/article/people-would-rather-be-electrically-shocked-left-alone-their-thoughts.

3. Kathleen Wong, "Survey Reveals Just What Europeans Really Think of American Tourists," *USA Today*, July 25, 2025, https://www.usatoday.com/story/travel/news/2025/07/24/american-tourist-reputation-european-study/85351608007.

4. Thomas Merton, *New Seeds of Contemplation* (Shambhala Publications, 2003), 85.

5. John Piper (@JohnPiper), Twitter (now X), October 20, 2009.

6. Evelyn Underhill, *The Mystics of the Church* (Wipf and Stock, 2002), 12–13.

7. James Finley, host, "Turning to Thomas Merton," *Turning to the Mystics*, podcast, season 1, episode 3, February 24, 2020.

8. Robert Barclay, *An Apology for the True Christian Divinity* (Quaker Heritage Press, 2002), http://www.qhpress.org/texts/barclay/apology/prop11.html.

9. Brother Lawrence, *The Practice of the Presence of God* (Whitaker House, 1982), 83–84.

10. F. B. Meyer, *The Secret of Guidance* (Christian Classical Ethereal Library), https://ccel.org/ccel/m/meyer/guidance/cache/guidance.pdf, 13.

11. *The Rule of St. Benedict* (Liturgical Press, 1980), prologue.

12. Richard J. Foster, *Celebration of Discipline* (HarperSanFrancisco, 1998), 173.

13. Joy Davidson, *Smoke on the Mountain: An Interpretation of the Ten Commandments* (Westminster, 1953), 133.

14. Peter Scazzero, *Emotionally Healthy Spirituality* (Zondervan, 2006), 146.

15. "The Eight Daily Prayer Periods," http://christdesert.org/prayer/opus-dei/the-eight-daily-prayer-periods.

16. Kosuke Koyama, *Three Mile an Hour God: Biblical Reflections* (Orbis, 1979), 6.

17. John Mark Comer, "Why Wasting Time with God Is What Our Hearts Need Most," Ann Voskamp, accessed February 8, 2026, https://annvoskamp.com/2024/01/why-wasting-time-with-god-is-what-our-hearts-need-most.

18. Robby Gallaty, *Rediscovering Discipleship* (Zondervan, 2015), 59.

19. A. W. Tozer, *The Root of the Righteous* (Moody, 2007), 23.

20. For further reading, see R. T. Kendall, *For an Audience of One* (Charisma House, 2020).

21. E. M. Bounds, *Power Through Prayer* (Whitaker House, 1982), 8.

22. Dominque Mosbergen, "People Really Do Look like Their Pets, and Here's Why," *Huffpost*, September 8, 2014. https://www.huffpost.com/entry/people-look-like-their-dogs-study_n_5838278.

23. Matthew Henry, *Matthew Henry's Commentary on the Whole Bible*, vol. 5, Matthew to John (Revell, 1975), 1145.

24. Michael Catt (@Michael Catt), Twitter (now X), August 16, 2018.

25. Amy Carmichael, *Candles in the Dark* (CLC Publications, 1982), 42.

26. George Duffield, "Stand Up, Stand Up for Jesus," public domain.

27. Anne Kerhoulas, "The Discipline of Remembering," Gospel Centered Discipleship, accessed February 11, 2026, https://gcdiscipleship.com/article-feed/the-discipline-of-remembering.

28. Thomas Merton, *Thoughts in Solitude* (Farrar, Strauss, and Cudahy, 1956), 33.

29. Peter Scazzero, *The Emotionally Healthy Leader* (Zondervan, 2015), 147.

30. Dallas Willard, *The Great Omission: Reclaiming Jesus's Essential Teachings on Discipleship* (Harper One, 2006), 61.

31. Erin Clements, "'Every single thing I know, as of today': author Anne Lamott shares life wisdom in viral Facebook post." *Today*, April 9, 2015, https://www.today.com/popculture/author-anne-lamott-shares-life-wisdom-viral-facebook-post-t13881.

32. For more of Pete's teaching on this subject, see "How to Grow a Flourishing Ministry without Losing Your Soul," *Emotionally Healthy Leader* podcast, season 10, episode 19, September 17, 2024.

33. Marty Solomon, host, "Trust the Story," *The BEMA Podcast*, season 1, episode 1, September 8, 2016.

34. Charles H. Spurgeon, "The High Rock," sermon preached March 23, 1859, The Spurgeon Center, https://www.spurgeon.org/resource-library/sermons/the-high-rock/#flipbook.

ABOUT THE AUTHOR

Robby Gallaty (MDiv, PhD, New Orleans Baptist Theological Seminary) is senior pastor of Long Hollow Church outside of Nashville, in Hendersonville, Tennessee. Radically saved in his twenties from a life of alcohol and drug addiction, his work has grown to include the founding of Replicate Ministries, a network of coaches who help churches create and contextualize their own disciple-making culture.

Among the many other books he's written are his autobiography, *Recovered*, titles like *Growing Up: How to Be a Disciple Who Makes Disciples*, and most recently, *Movement-Ready Church*, with coauthor Vick Green. He's also collaborated with his wife, Kandi, on *The Practice of Prayer* and a number of *Foundations* Bible studies. They have two boys: Rig and Ryder.